Carolina Wine Country

The Complete Guide

Pamela Watson

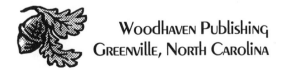

Woodhaven Publishing
GREENVILLE, NORTH CAROLINA

Carolina Wine Country *The Complete Guide* Copyright © 1999 by Pamela Watson

Published by:

Woodhaven Publishing
104 Woodhaven Court
Greenville, North Carolina 27834 - 6930
(252) 353-2800
(877) 353-2800 (toll free)
Web site: www.NCBooks.com

ISBN 0-9667116-0-2

Library of Congress Catalog Card Number: 98-96635

All care has been taken to assure that the information contained in this book, including addresses, telephone numbers, web sites, e-mail addresses and all content, is complete and correct. However, owing to the fast pace of our Tele-connected world, these items sometimes change faster than it is possible to keep up with them. The author and publisher assume no responsibility for errors, inaccuracies, omissions, or inconsistencies. Any slights of people, places, or organizations are unintentional.

The articles concerning wine and health are not an endorsement for drinking wine or any other alcoholic beverage. Their purpose is to introduce some of the research being done into the relationship of wine and heart, and other diseases. For further readings on the subject, refer to the footnotes and the bibliography of this book. Consult your doctor before making any changes regarding your lifestyle and the consumption of alcohol.

Note: No one should consume alcohol and operate motor vehicles or machinery. It is not only unsafe, it is unlawful. Likewise, people with problematic drinking in their family histories should avoid alcohol. Be safe, be smart. Don't drink and drive.

To my mother-in-law,
Muriel,
with whom I sip sherry;

To my mother,
Patty Ann,
we laugh, and drink rosé;

To the memory of my father-in-law,
Don,
who argued with the waitress
(and won)
over whether or not the
Piesporter was cold enough;

And to my father,
Joe,
who passed away during the
writing of this book, and on whom I
forced a number of wines over the
years. He'd nod and say,
"That's pretty good," but his next
round would always be a beer.

Books By Pamela Watson

99 Fun Things To Do In Columbia and Boone County (Missouri)
(available from Pebble Publishing (800) 576-7322)

Carolina Wine Country The Complete Guide
Alamance to Zebulon: ABC's of North Carolina Place Names
(available summer 1999)

Photo Credits

Front cover, Rachael Watson

Back cover: aerial photo of the French Broad River courtesy of Biltmore Estate, Asheville, North Carolina; Truluck Vineyards horsebarn and author photo, Nick Watson

The woodcut of the Medoc Vineyards Wine Cellar (page 17) and the photo of the Garrett & Company Winery (page 19), courtesy of the North Carolina Collection, University of North Carolina Library at Chapel Hill.

The photos of the old Scuppernong Vine (page 14) and Mahler's Vineyard (page 21) courtesy of the N. C. Division of Archives and History.

The photos of the picnic in the vineyard (page 6), Biltmore winery (page 108) and Biltmore grape harvest (page 111) courtesy of Biltmore Estate, Asheville, North Carolina.

Ferry logo reproduced with permission of the North Carolina Department of Transportation.

Scuppernong grapes (page 26), barrels at Westbend Vineyards (page 71), and the woman with Scuppernongs (page 184) courtesy of the North Carolina Grape Council.

Horseback riding in the Smokies (page 127) courtesy of the Haywood County Tourism Development Authority.

The Revolutionary War soldier (page 136) and the Catawba Cultural Center (page 137) courtesy of the Olde English District Tourism Commission.

The Aiken Historical Museum (page 146) and the Steeplechase (page 149) courtesy of Thoroughbred Country, Aiken, South Carolina.

The photograph of Mr. And Mrs. Ray Stamm (page 166) courtesy of Crescent Mountain Vineyards.

Photos by Rachael Watson (pages 11, 84, 86, 87, 92, 95, 100, 102, 118, 120)
Photos by Nick Watson (pages 35, 39, 123, 160, 162, 164)
All other photos by Pamela Watson

I'm not out here on my own. Without the assistance, advice and suggestions of many wonderful people, this book would never have seen the inside of my computer, much less the surface of a bookstore shelf.

Too many thank-yous to count go to Tania Dautlick, Executive Director of the North Carolina Grape Council for her advice and suggestions. From the very beginning, she accepted my phone calls and e-mails with patience, professionalism and warmth. Both the Carolina wine industry and I owe her an unlimited debt of gratitude.

Without the grape growers, the wine makers, and the winery owners themselves, there would be no Carolina Wine Country *The Complete Guide*. They were all wonderfully patient , answering my questions (some pretty ignorant ones in the beginning), and taking time from their busy schedules to share their stories, and show me their vineyards and wineries. Thank you all so much.

Thanks to Steve Massengil at the Division of Archives and History of the North Carolina Department of Cultural Resources for helping me find some great old photographs for History of the Grape. He sent me on to Jerry Cotten at the University of North Carolina Library at Chapel Hill, who helped me find a few more. I thank you both; I'd never have found them on my own.

Thanks to Stephen Lyons, Vineyard Design & Management Consultant in Columbus, NC who put me in the right direction for the Wineries To Be.

Thanks to everyone along the way who had words of encouragement and positive responses. To Faye and Don Dempsey, and Kelly Fleming who'd ask, "How's your wine book coming along?"; to Carolyn Wilburn of the SBTDC who thought it was a great idea, and to my Mom and my Mum for having faith in me.

Last, but far from least, thank you to my terrific family who endured no meals and a messy house (not that I'm a great housekeeper anyway, but I'm always worse when I'm writing a book), and me being a little more neurotic than normal for ten months. To Rachael, my sounding wall, who listened to all my ups and downs on a daily basis and who still managed to be supportive and interested. To Gwen, who puts up with me being weird anyway, but who always had a "Good job, Mom!" handy when needed. And to my wonderful husband, Nick, who for 24 years has believed in me. That and cheesecake is all I need in life.

"Good wine is a necessity of life."
- Thomas Jefferson

Table of Contents

Wineries To Be

*It's a naïve domestic Burgundy
without any breeding,
but I think you'll be amused
by its presumption.*
Cartoon caption in *New Yorker* (27 March 1937)
- James Thurber (1894–1961),
U.S. humorist, illustrator.

North Carolina Grapes and Wine

By Tania Dautlick

Executive Director, North Carolina Grape Council

Many people have taken the journey into grape growing, wine making, and wine appreciation. For North Carolinians, this journey began in the sixteenth century when European explorers like Giovanni de Verrazano and Sir Walter Raleigh discovered native muscadine grapes growing on the pristine coastal lands of what is now the Outer Banks.

Settlers began making wine with these grapes, as their families had done for generations in their home lands. Native North Carolina grapes sustained the national wine industry into the early twentieth century. A high point occurred in 1904 when a Carolina muscadine wine, Virginia Dare produced by Paul Garrett, won the grand prize in the Louisiana Purchase Exhibition. This notoriety lasted until Prohibition in 1919.

North Carolina vineyards and wineries came and went as the tides changed and consumer interest in wine fluctuated. In 1972 the State Legislature passed a preferential state excise tax law that was designed to foster the establishment of a wine industry in North Carolina. Wines produced from 51% or more native fruits and berries were taxed at five cents per gallon as opposed to 60 cents per gallon for all other wines.

Families throughout the state planted vineyards and opened wineries utilizing this incentive. Vineyards in the east continued to make wine based on the native muscadines, while enterprising growers in the Piedmont and mountains discovered that European grapes would prosper at higher elevations with special care. Unfortunately, the state lost its preferential tax rate in 1985 following the U.S. Supreme Court's decision in the "Bacchus Case" which declared such laws to be a violation of the freedom of commerce clause of the U.S. Constitution.

In 1986 the North Carolina Grape Growers Association, under the guidance of Jeff Morton of the North Carolina Department of Agriculture, led an effort to create the North Carolina Grape Council. Legislation was introduced and Senate Bill 994 was ratified in 1986 to create the 11-member council. The mission is to facilitate growth and assure quality of the North Carolina grape and wine industry through education, marketing and research. Funding was provided for the council in 1987 with the passage of Senate Bill 164, which diverts to the council a portion of the state's excise tax on wine bottled in North Carolina.

The North Carolina Grape Council has since taken the lead in developing new varieties of grapes that will withstand the variable climates in the state. In addition to sponsoring grape breeding research, the Grape

Council assists grape growers through research which improves vineyard techniques, addresses storage and processing concerns for fresh grapes, and strives for high quality North Carolina grapes and wines. Grape growing and wine making today is a profitable and popular practice for North Carolinians. Vineyards produce a high return per acre and preserve picturesque farmland, while wineries make value-added products to benefit the state economy and the tourism trade.

The Council promotes discovery and responsible wine enjoyment through marketing and educational projects. With a focus to increase consumer awareness of North Carolina grapes, the Council sponsors wine tasting events, festivals and grape stomps, and produces a variety of educational materials. Consumers may contact the Council for winery and vineyard locations or special grape recipes, among other grape-related information.

The North Carolina Grape Council applauds the thorough coverage given to the wineries and vineyards of the Carolinas in this book. This work is a direct extension of the educational efforts of the Council. As you, too, embark on a journey into the world of vineyards and wineries, the North Carolina Grape Council welcomes you to experience for yourself this wonderful discovery.

From the Mountains to the Sea
An Introduction to the Wine Country

When asked what was her favorite wine, the lady replied, "The one I'm drinking now." That pretty well describes my attitude toward wine. Since the days when my room mate and I put our left over coins together to buy whatever wine we could afford, my tastes have run the length and breadth of vino offerings. From cheap "soda-pop" reds, to classic German whites; from wine coolers to wines so dry they bite you; I can't say I've tried them all, but I've made a good start.

The so-called wine experts would have us all believe that there is something about wine that is beyond the understanding of the common person. Yet, through the ages, wine has been the common drink of all classes of people. From Biblical times to the present, wine has been used to celebrate, seduce, honor, and interrogate. Wine is made by home hobby-vintners and 10th generation Wine Masters. It is consumed by newlyweds following their vows and adversaries following the signing of a peace treaty. Wine is part of our culture. It is part of who we are.

It should be no surprise, then, to find that wine has been produced in the Carolinas since the first English settlers set up house keeping. The wild Muscadine grapes were so abundant in the colonies that it seemed every plot of land came with vines. Prior to the Civil War, North Carolina was the leading wine producing state in the country. However, the war, Re-construction, and Prohibition all left their marks on the industry well into the mid 20th Century. Between the 1940's and the 1960's only a few wineries opened, operated for a while, then closed.

Then in the 1970's two wineries on opposite ends of the state and producing very different kinds of wines opened for business; Biltmore Estate Winery in the mountains and Duplin Wine Cellars near the coast. While Biltmore cultivated French vinifera grapes, Duplin chose the native Muscadines and Scuppernongs. Today, both wineries have thriving businesses and loyal customers. Both wineries continue to be the backbone of the growing Carolina Wine industry, making North Carolina once again a contender on the national scene at 10th in the nation in wine production.

This book was a natural project, then, for a travel and history writer who likes wine. Here was a whole wide, wonderful world of wines and wineries, people and history, located in some of the most beautiful country on earth just waiting for me to explore. My goal was to visit every winery in the Carolinas, eleven in North Carolina, and five in South Carolina, and I'm happy to report I did it! I crossed waterways on the ferries, hiked trails in state and national parks, and visited historic sites and homes. I traveled more than 5000 miles and never left the Carolinas. I met the most interesting people whose love of growing grapes and making wines keep them going, even through bad years of Black Rot and hurricanes, drought and changing liquor laws. I also sampled lots of wonderful wines.

The North Carolina Grape Council calls Carolina Wine Country a Variety Vineland. It truly is. You can visit Silohouse, our western most vineyard and winery in Waynesville near the Great Smokey Mountains and find a Cabernet Sauvignon that matches the scenery. Arrive at Martin Vineyards on Knotts Island on the Outer Banks and sample a peach wine that is as romantic as the ferry ride. Montmorenci Vineyards in Thoroughbred Country near Aiken, South Carolina offers a robust Chambourcin that invites you to toss the steaks on the grill and kick back and enjoy the evening. Each winery is different and each wine maker as unique as his or her wines. If wine is the extension of the vintner's soul, then know these vintners by the wines they make.

This book is for families, couples, singles, wine lovers and people who have never tasted wine. It is for armchair travelers, seasoned travelers, and people who want to go somewhere for a Saturday outing. Visit a winery, or choose a U-pick vineyard and spend a morning picking your own grapes. Bring the children, bring a picnic, bring the camera. Explore.

Can't get away? Head for the kitchen and cook up some of the recipes, or create crafts from wine corks and bottles. Go on-line and explore Carolina Wine Country in cyberspace. Several of the wineries have excellent web pages. The North Carolina Grape Council has a super one as well with lots of juicy links. A number of wineries are working on web pages even now, so happy surfing.

The book is divided it into states, and sections within each state to help you locate each winery geographically. Spend as much time as you wish exploring the nearby history, shopping, and outdoor activities. There's also a chapter entitled "Ideas For Touring" to help you plan a Carolina Wine Country trip, or you can start by visiting the winery nearest you and explore the others when you have the time.

Please take note that when crossing state lines, private consumers are allowed to carry up to 20 liters of table wine with them. That's a little over two cases. Many states have laws limiting the shipping of wine, and both North and South Carolina are in that category. Wine makers can ship wines within their state, and to other states if those states are not on the "no ship" list, so ask at the winery about your state. "No ship" states include North Carolina, South Carolina, Florida, Georgia, and Virginia. Hopefully, in the near future, these laws will be changed and wine can enjoy fair interstate commerce along with other agricultural products. For more information on legal issues affecting the wine industry, go to the North Carolina Grape Council's web site at:
www.agr.state.nc.us/markets/commodit/horticul/grape/legal.htm

I tried to make Carolina Wine Country, The Complete Guide, as comprehensive as possible. Addresses, telephone numbers, web sites and e-mail addresses were all checked and double checked, but at the rate of speed that our world is changing, I can't guarantee that what was correct yesterday will still be so tomorrow. If you find outdated numbers or closed businesses, please let me know. Equally, if you find new things that you think should be added to the Wine Country, tell me, and we can include them in the next edition.

It was a tough job, but somebody had to do it. Somebody had to explore two of the prettiest states in the union and drink all that wine so that you, gentle reader could have this information at your fingertips. Now it's your turn. Try a new wine, travel a new road. Explore Carolina Wine Country. See for yourself the beauty, the fun, the history and the people of this fabulous Variety Vineland, from the mountains to the sea.

Pamela Watson
Greenville, North Carolina
1998

"Old Scuppernong Vine" in Roanoke, North Carolina, circa 1900.
Legend has it that this is the 350 year old "Mother-vine"

With the growth of the grape every
nation elevates itself to a higher
grade of civilization.
- Friedrich Muench 1798-1881
School for American Grape Culture

History of the Grape - Part I

Long before people distilled spirits, they fermented fruit. It probably started accidentally when a caveman named Grog forgot about the wild grapes he'd picked in the forest. When he finally got around to opening the hollow log he'd stored them in, his grapes had burst, the flowing juice and natural sugars producing a pleasant drink, with just a hint of oak. Grog liked it, so he picked more grapes and let them burst. Gradually he watched Nature process the fruit and learned to manipulate the activity using different grapes and creating different flavors. Grog spread the word and soon everyone was making the grape drinks.

Fast forward several thousand years and you find that during all this time wine continued to be enjoyed the world over. In the 16th and 17th centuries when European explorers were busily searching for new lands to plunk their counties' flags into, they were ever mindful of the natural resources and what could be produced from them. In the New World, it was found that grapes grew naturally and abundantly. Sure, you could eat them but better yet, you could drink them.

In 1524, Giovanni de Verrazano, a Florentine navigator sailing under the flag of France, reached the coast of present day North Carolina. While exploring the area of the Cape Fear River Valley, he recorded in his logbook that he saw, "many vines growing naturally there that without doubt would yield excellent wines." Unfortunately for de Verrazano, he never returned to the land of the grape. He was killed by natives in 1527 while exploring the coast of Brazil.

In 1584, Sir Walter Raleigh, riding high on a wave of royal popularity, was anxious to establish an English colony in the New World. It certainly couldn't hurt in keeping the Queen's favor. He sent Captains Phillip Amadas and Arthur Barlowe over to check out the Real Estate. When they reached the North Carolina coast, they were overwhelmed by what they saw. They wrote in their logbook:

"The North Carolina coast was so full of grapes that the very beating and surge of the sea overflowed them. They covered every shrub and climbed the tops of high cedars. In all the world, a similar abundance was not to be found. Their smell of sweetness filled the air as if they were in the midst of some delicate garden."

Sir Walter's colony was established on Roanoke Island in 1587. Legend has it that a huge grapevine, called the Mother-vine, was on the island and the colonists were able to gather grapes and make wine. All seemed happy in the colony. There was even a new baby, the first baby born in the New World. Her name was Virginia Dare. However, when the supply ship returned in 1590 everyone had mysteriously vanished without a trace and the Lost Colony remains a mystery today.

However, owing to other circumstances, namely his secret marriage to one of Queen Elizabeth's ladies in waiting, Sir Walter found himself out of royal favor by 1592. He did not attempt to colonize the New World again.

In 1663, King Charles II granted the Carolina territory to eight proprietors who divided it into North and South Carolina. In its Latin form, *Carolinus* means "of Charles", the territory having been named for Charles I and Charles II. The abundance of grapes as reported by the early explorers was not an exaggeration. Wild grapes grew everywhere along the coast. Wherever a settler staked his claim, he usually found he had an established vineyard that came with the property. Furthermore, the grapes were like nothing the Europeans had ever seen before. They were *Vitis rotundifolia*, round grapes, native only to the southern states. We know them by the common name of Muscadine. One variety, simply called the "large white grape," seemed particularly well suited for wine making. By the time of the American Revolution, wine making was well established among the residents of eastern North Carolina.

On January 11, 1811 an article written by Dr. Calvin Jones appeared in the Raleigh *Star* under the heading "North Carolina Wine from Native Grapes." In it, Jones commented on the recent census report of Washington County submitted by James Blount of the town of Scuppernong. Blount reported that in 1810, 1,368 gallons of wine were made from a locally grown large white grape, an amount extensive enough to qualify as a new American industry. After mentioning the size, color and taste of the grape, the article stated that it had been cultivated for a number of years in the vicinity of Phelps Lake near Scuppernong. It also briefly outlined the local process of wine making, one part brandy to three parts juice; fortified wine and probably with a powerful kick. For want of a better name, Jones called the grape Scuppernong.

The Scuppernong grape has a tough skin that is bronzy green in color and is, to use the traditional Tarheel description, about the size of a "hog's eye." As with all Muscadines, the fruit grows in clusters rather than in bunches, and when ripe can be easily shaken off the vine. The word *scuppernong* comes from *askuponong* in the Southern Algonquain language which means "in the country of the sweet bay tree". These "bay trees" or "bay laurels" grow in the magnolia swamps of eastern North Carolina, specifically in the area south of the Albemarle Sound.

In 1817, patriot, ex-president, and wine connoisseur, Thomas Jefferson secured a barrel of unfortified Scuppernong wine from a source in Washington County. He quickly declared it a superb specimen and it became one of his favorites. In a letter to his good friend William Johnson dated May 10, 1817, Jefferson stated:

" North Carolina has the merit of taking the lead in the former culture, of giving the first specimen of an exquisite wine, produced in quantity, and established in it's culture beyond the danger of being discontinued. Her Scuppernon (as he spelled it) wine, made on the South side of the Sound, would be distinguished on the best tables of Europe, for its fine aroma and crystalline transparence."

However, just because he was Thomas Jefferson didn't mean he could necessarily get what he wanted. He had a terrible time getting more of it and sent his grandson, Francis Eppes, to Washington County to negotiate the sale. In a letter dated October 31, 1822, Eppes wrote to Jefferson:

"I obtained from Col. Burton the address of several gentlemen who make the Carolina wine. He was much opposed to giving the information being willing and indeed anxious to procure it for you, but upon my insisting told me that Thomas Cox & Co. Commission Merchants Plymouth, would be more likely to please than any others. The makers of the wine are persons in easy circumstances, who do not care to oblige, generally keeping the best for themselves."

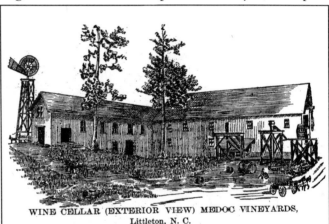

WINE CELLAR (EXTERIOR VIEW) MEDOC VINEYARDS, Littleton, N. C.

Col. Burton knew a distributor's percentage when he saw it, but there was the added problem that these private wine makers were wealthy enough not to worry if they sold their wine or not - and, what they did sell wasn't their best wine. However, Jefferson finally found a reliable distributor, and he also became interested in cultivating Scuppernong vines among the many varieties he grew at Monticello. Unfortunately, he was not successful.

Wine making in North Carolina continued to thrive. Twenty five wineries were established prior to the Civil War. The first of these commercial ventures was Medoc Vineyards in Halifax County, started in 1835 by Sidney Weller. By 1840, Medoc was the largest in the state with six acres of vineyards producing 1500 to 3600 gallons per year. Among other things, the War Between the States disrupted wine making in the South and sent many vintners heading North until it could all blow over.

In the latter part of the 19th century, wine making was once again a booming industry in North Carolina. Places such as Happy Valley Vineyard near Fayetteville, Engadine Vineyard in Buncombe County, Niagara Vineyard in Southern Pines, Castle Hayne Vineyard, the Bordeaux Vineyard and Tokay Vineyard Winery, also near Fayetteville produced thousands of gallons of scuppernong wine annually.

The most successful of these 19th century grape barons was a doctor's son named Paul Garrett. Garrett grew up on the Medoc Vineyards after his uncle, Charles Garrett, bought the property in 1867 and renamed it Ringwood Wine Company. Along with a military academy education, young Paul learned the vineyard business from the ground up, so to speak. At the age of 14, he learned bookkeeping as well as the production aspects of the grape and wine business with the belief that he would one day take over management of the company.

When Charles Garrett died, however, one of his sons-in-law of was put in charge. He and young Paul didn't see eye to eye, so Paul went on the road as a traveling salesman for Ringwood. Eventually, the young entrepreneur struck out on his own, establishing Garrett & Company in 1900. Like any good legendary folk hero who's had his birthright wrenched from him, he was later vindicated when he bought out Ringwood Wine Company and added it to his growing empire.

Paul Garrett knew the wine business and he knew what people liked. Furthermore, he knew how to market, and market he did. He played to exactly what the romantic Victorians loved; tragic stories of love, loss and unsolved mysteries. He called his pure Scuppernong wine Virginia Dare. Remember the Lost Colony? He traded on the romance of the long lost child and her fellow colonists, and of the historical aspects of the so called "Mother-vine." He gave his other wines the romantic Indian names of the day, Minnehaha and Hiawatha. He kept his wine on the nation's tongues as well as its tables. At the 1904 Louisiana Purchase Exhibition in St. Louis, Missouri, Virginia Dare took the grand prize.

However, the popularity of the wine caused production problems for Garrett. There simply weren't enough Scuppernong grapes being grown to accommodate the demand, but that didn't stop him. Gradually he started blending other grapes into Virginia Dare, retaining enough Scuppernongs to maintain the unique flavor.

In 1905, Garrett published a small but powerful booklet entitled *The Art of Serving Wine*. It included the how, when and what kinds of wines to serve, the "etiquette of the glass" and persuasive arguments that wine is

Paul Garrett & Company winery, circa 1890

a real food, a health-giving joy and a cure for the "liquor evil." The booklet also contained a description of the Scuppernong grape along with its connections with Roanoke Island. To enhance the history, Garrett included a long narrative poem in the style of Longfellow and written by Mrs. Sallie Southall Cotton entitled *The White Doe: The Fate of Virginia Dare*. The booklet was a huge success. Sales of Virginia Dare wine soared and Garrett became very wealthy. His trademark, blown into the glass of all his bottles carried a picture of an eagle, wings outstretched, hovering over a cluster of Scuppernongs bordered by Confederate battle flags and bearing the words "Garrett's American Wines".

By the time World War I sent American dough boys to the fox-holes, Paul Garrett had an empire of farms and wineries that stretched from North Carolina to Virginia to New York, to Ohio, to Missouri to California. Virginia Dare was the largest selling wine in the country. The Volstead Act of 1919, commonly called Prohibition, put an end to post war wine and cheese parties. The cork was back in the bottle.

Undaunted, Garrett tried several ways to keep his empire going. He formed a company for the purpose of marketing juice concentrate for home wine making. Several other copy-cat companies caught onto the idea. So did the government.

Garrett also had his wine maker add beef extract, pepsin, and a variety of other ingredients to his hidden stores of Virginia Dare wine, which he then sold off as Virginia Dare Tonic. Alcohol was legal as a medicine. Sacramental wines and wines for other religious purposes were also legal, so Garrett continued to produce these.

Being a creative businessman, Garrett didn't twiddle his thumbs while waiting out Prohibition, so when repeal came in 1933, he was the only vintner ready to produce wine again. However, now the country was in the depths of the Great Depression, but once again Paul Garrett was ready with his own recovery plan. Have the people grow grapes (particularly Scuppernong grapes). He pushed the idea at every Federal agency he could, but, with "Dry" sentiments still prevalent in the South, it just never took off. He continued to produce Virginia Dare with limited quantities of Scuppernongs and relying on juice from his California vineyards. Despite the fact that Garrett introduced the first ever singing radio commercial in 1933, and continued to market heavily, Virginia Dare had lost its appeal.

Paul Garrett died on March 18, 1940 at the age of 76. With no surviving heir, his wine empire went with him. Many believe that he was ahead of his time in predicting that America would become a great wine producing and wine drinking nation. He is still considered America's most productive, largest selling, most creative and most tireless wine maker.

From 1950 to the early 1970's several commercial wine makers came and went in North Carolina. A number of vineyardists began growing Scuppernongs as out of state wineries offered to pay as much as $200.00 per ton for the grapes. In 1955, one of these growers, Raymond Hartsfield, decided to open a winery. He called it Onslow Wine Cellars which he operated until 1968 when he sold out to Richard Wine Cellars in Petersburg, Virginia. In 1974, Deerfield Vineyards Wine Cellars was opened by George Wood near Edenton. It operated successfully for six years, producing 55,000 gallons of estate bottled wine in 1980. It closed with Wood's death that same year.

History of the Grape - Part II

North Carolina's modern wine industry began with the opening of two wineries in the 1970's that still operate today, Biltmore Estate Winery and Duplin Wine Cellars. In 1973 the New River Grape Grower's Association which had formed in 1962 changed its name to the North Carolina Grape Grower's Association. Research began at the University of North Carolina to determine what other grape varieties could be grown in the state. Although Muscadines continue to grow well in the coastal areas, experiments with French and American hybrids in the upcountry have proven successful. In 1986, through a legislative act, the North Carolina Grape Council was formed to stimulate the expansion of North Carolina's grape and wine industry by funding research studies and marketing and promotional efforts. Today, North Carolina is known as much for its Seyval as for its Scuppernong.

North Carolina is the home of our nation's first cultivated wine grape. It continues to promote growth and sale of a number of varieties of grapes and wine. Every time you try a new wine, you're adding to the history of this most diverse and universal of beverages. So take the plunge into North Carolina's Variety Vineland. Paul Garrett would Dare you - and then sell you the wine.

Mahler's Vineyard near Raleigh, NC, circa 1900.

Drink a Glass of Wine
After Your Soup
and You Steal a Ruble
from Your Doctor.
- Russian Proverb

Wine - The Miracle Elixir?

S *tep right up ladies and gentlemen, don't be shy. What I have here is the miracle beverage of the ages. Consumed by kings and commoners alike. The cure to all your aches and pains, worries and stresses. Just one glass a day will keep you in the pink of health and send the doctor on his way. And what is this potent potion, you ask?. Well, it's wine my friend, pure juice of the grape, fruit of the vine, the elixir of life. Vino veritas.*

Fortunately we don't have to endure that sales pitch in order to enjoy a glass of wine, but the truth is that over the past ten years, dozens of scientific studies have found that a glass of wine, either red or white, each day with your meal, reduces the risk of heart attack and other diseases. There is evidence as well that moderate drinking (described as one to two glasses per day) may increase estrogen levels in post-menopausal women (1), reduce the risk of some cancers (2), reduce the risk of kidney stones (3), gallstones (4), osteoporosis (5), non-insulin dependent diabetes (6), and effectively wipe out several types of bacteria that often lead to food poisoning, diarrhea (7), and hepatitis A (8). Could wine truly be the miracle elixir of all time?

Historically, wine has been recommended for the treatment of iron deficiency anemia ("A little wine will build up your blood."), sleep disorders ("A glass of wine before bedtime will help you sleep better."), and stress ("Have a glass of sherry, dear. It will calm your nerves."). It has been prescribed for upset stomachs, to aid digestion and to help increase the absorption of minerals and nutrients. Much of this advice has been attributed to "old wives tales" or folk medicine, but on November 17, 1991, the television news show *60 Minutes* aired a story that sent both the health gurus and the wine industry reeling. Citing work done by Dr. Serge Renaud, Director of Research at Lyon, France-based INSERM (the equivalent of the U. S. National Institute of Health) and Dr. Curt Ellison, Chief of Epidemiology, Boston University, 60 Minutes reported that wine may be the reason the French live longer. They called it the French Paradox .

What Renaud and Ellis found was that the French develop coronary heart disease at less than half the rate of that of Americans. Yet, the French eat foods high in fat, exercise less than Americans and have heavy smoking habits. The researchers concluded that the French custom of drinking wine each day with meals was a possible explanation for the difference. Since then, a number of studies have drawn the same conclusion and show that moderate alcohol consumption is associated with a 20% to 40% reduction in the risk of coronary heart disease.

There appear to be several reasons for this risk reduction. One is that moderate consumption seems to increase levels of HDL (high density lipoprotein), what scientists call good cholesterol, and decreases level of LDL (low density lipoprotein) or bad cholesterol. HDL reduces heart disease risk by helping to clear cholesterol from arteries and eliminate it from the body. LDL potentially increases the risk because it breaks up easily, allowing cholesterol deposits to circulate in the blood and stick to artery walls.

Second, alcohol appears to help counteract the tendency of platelets, a type of blood cell, to form clots that may lead to blocked arteries. Third, and most importantly, researchers have discovered that the phenolic compounds in wine, which includes tannins, act as powerful antioxidants when absorbed into the bloodstream. These antioxidants inhibit the formation of certain kinds of blood clots that can lead to heart attacks.

An important factor to keep in mind, the scientists are quick to point out, is that although the French consume more wine that any nation on earth, they do so daily with meals. Americans tend to binge drink. If you have three bottles of wine all on Saturday night, it's bad for your blood, arteries, heart and health in general. But, if you spread out those three bottles and have half a bottle each day with a leisurely meal, you may well be doing your heart a favor.

On November 5, 1995, 60 Minutes did a follow-up story with even more shocking news. They reported the findings of a 12 year study in Denmark called the Copenhagen Heart Study. The research involved more than 13,000 men and women between the ages of 30 and 79 and compared beer, wine, liquor and abstinence. The results showed that those who abstained from alcohol had a 37% higher risk of dying from any cause than those who had one drink per day. Furthermore, wine drinkers, more than drinkers of beer or distilled spirits, showed the lowest risk of mortality.*

The findings indicate that, although alcohol plays a role in reduction of mortality risk, alcohol alone is not the answer. It is the presence of the antioxidants that makes the difference. Furthermore, excessive alcohol, 3 to 5 drinks or more per day, can cause cancers, sclerosis of the liver and other problems of alcoholism. It is the pattern of drinking with meals, on a daily basis in the European fashion, as opposed to the typical American pattern of binge drinking on the weekends and not drinking in between that are the major factors, say the scientists. It's the pattern and not the amount of alcohol that is important.

So, go ahead and have that glass of wine with dinner. It doesn't matter if it's red or white. Research shows that both have the same heart protecting capabilities. But if you prefer your wine in a capsule form, your local health food store is sure to have wine-grape extracts in stock. One French company, Arkopharm markets skins and seeds ground into pill form and more supplements are coming on the market each day. So step right up ladies and gentlemen and get your daily dose for a healthy heart. As for me, I prefer mine liquid.

(1) Gavaler, University of Pittsburgh; Journal of Alcoholism, March 1992
(2) Boffetta and Garfinkel; Journal of Epidemiology 1990
(3) Curhan, G. et al. Journal of Epidemiology 1996
(4) LaVecchia, C. International Journal for Vitamin and Nutrition Research, 1994
(5) Barrett-Bonnor, E., British Medical Journal, 1993
(6) Rimm, EB et al. British Medical Journal, 1995
(7) Weisse, M. et al. British Medical Journal, 1995
(8) Center for Disease Control and Florida Department of Health and Rehabilitative Services; Epidemiology, July 1992

* For a complete transcript of the November 5, 1995 report on 60 Minutes, go to http://smartwine.com/fp/60mintrs.htm on the Internet.

"Drink no longer water,
but use a little wine
for thy stomach's sake
and thine often infirmities."
- Bible, 1 Timothy 5.23

NC's Favorite Grape May Be Good for the Heart

By Sarah Avery

Rose Hill, North Carolina –

I n the aristocratic world of wine grapes, North Carolina's native muscadine long has been the plebeian cousin to such noble European Vitis as chardonnays and pinots noir. Alas, ours has been an earthy, sweet fruit to their heady, piquant bouquets. We grow sandhills Scuppernong; they raise sovereign Sauvignon.

Yeah, well sip on this, Beaujolais breath: Our grape might be better after all. That's right. The Muscadine rules when it comes to a little something that might make wine good for the heart. In a preliminary study released in August (1996) to the state's wine growers, a Campbell University biologist found that our native Muscadines have the highest concentration of a molecule suspected of being a key cholesterol-cutting ingredient in wine.

"If this thing pans out, then obviously the people who have been drinking muscadine wine will be happy," said David Ohashi, a professor of pharmaceutical sciences at Campbell University.

Those happy people could get the last laugh within months if Ohashi and his colleagues prove their thesis, which builds on a growing base of scientific evidence that moderate wine consumption is good for the heart.

Evidence of wine's healthful qualities came in the early 1990's, when scientists discovered that wine-drinking people in northern France had little heart disease, even though they ate a lot of fatty foods. Scientists found that the paradox could be traced to their consumption of red wine, which contains a natural combination of ingredients that increase food cholesterol levels while reducing bad. That finding prompted some health officials to declare that a person who drinks a moderate amount of red wine every day would be doing his heart a favor.

While scientists aren't sure what it is about red wine that makes it so helpful to the heart, they suspect it has something to do with a powerful antioxidant called resveratrol, which shows up in small quantities. And that's where the Muscadine wines come barreling in.

Ohashi wondered how native North Carolina wines rated for resveratrol. What he found was significant: concentrations of the molecule in the state's Muscadine wines are up to seven times higher that those in the fancy European vintages. And not only is resveratrol evident in red Muscadine; it's there in the whites, too. Such high concentrations of resveratrol might be attributable to the very climatic conditions that make growing high-toned European grapes difficult in Eastern North Carolina: Lots of heat and high humidity.

Non-native grapes can't take Tar Heel summers; they rot. But the tough-skinned Muscadines do just fine, and it might be elevated levels of resveratrol that keep them healthy.

Ohashi is continuing his analysis this year at Campbell with a $3,000 grant from the North Carolina Grape Council. And while he cautions that his results are preliminary, the state's muscadine growers and winemakers can scarcely contain their glee.

"This is the most exciting thing I've come across in the 24 years I've been messing with grapes," said David Fussell, who owns Duplin Wine Cellars, the state's largest Muscadine winery.
Fussell said the prospects are enormous if further studies prove that the state's native grape is to heart disease what the orange was to scurvy.

Already, he said, interest in resveratrol has carved out a small but significant market for even Muscadine garbage. He says his winery sold 15 tons of pressed seeds and skins that otherwise have no value to pharmaceutical companies last year.

Terry Bland, an N. C. State University agricultural extension officer who works with Muscadines, said that as more and more studies confirm the grape's healthful qualities, demand for Muscadine wines - and perhaps jellies and juices as well - will increase.

"It does show promise," Bland said. "Nobody wants to be tied down on this until more studies come through, but I am excited about it."

Fussell already is banking on the news. Until now, he has concentrated on making wine, using grapes purchased from other growers. But this year, he'll plant 10 acres of his own vines. It's a hefty gamble; the plants require weekly tending for three years before producing a marketable product.

"I think growing grapes in North Carolina," Fussell said, "could become the alternative crop to tobacco."

Reprinted with permission of The News & Observer of Raleigh, North Carolina, August 19, 1996

"Wine is sure proof that God loves us and wants us to be happy!"

- Benjamin Franklin

North Carolina
The Coast

NORTH CAROLINA FERRY SYSTEM

1-800-BY FERRY

Ferry Facts

North Carolina Ferry System
1-800-BY-FERRY (1-800-293-3779) toll free for a free brochure of ferry routes and departure times.
Web site: www.dot.state.nc.us/transit/ferry

Ferries have plied the rivers and sounds of North Carolina since the mid-1920's. Originally these ferries were privately own and operated, delivering much needed goods and medical supplies to the coastal communities of Eastern North Carolina. They also provided a quicker way to get from one peninsula to another without going miles around on the roadways.

In 1934, the state of North Carolina saw the need for continuing ferry transportation and began subsidizing the private operators. In 1947, the North Carolina Ferry Division was established under the auspices of the North Carolina Transportation Department. Today, North Carolina has one of the largest ferry systems in the country, transporting more than 2.3 million people annually.

A ferry ride is an adventure in itself. You'll see wildlife, pristine coasts and romantic sunsets. In exploring Carolina Wine Country, there are several opportunities for you to ride the ferry. Although in going to Martin Vineyard on Knotts Island you can avoid the ferry by going up into Virginia and down on State Road 615, you'll miss the adventure of seeing the Corolla lighthouse across the Currituck Sound.

Don't forget to stop in at the ferry store before you leave. Several of the larger vessels have stores on board and stores are located at the terminals at Cedar Island, Ocracoke, Hatteras, Swan Quarter, Southport, Pamlico River and Cherry Branch. You can purchase t-shirts, sweatshirts, hats, coffee/travel mugs, magnets and key chains, all with the distinctive NC Ferry logo and in nautical colors. You can also pick up ferry schedules, maps, brochures of local attractions and bumper stickers.

Fun Ferry Facts

The North Carolina Ferry Division operates 24 ferry vessels, one dredge and numerous support vessels.

There are seven routes in the North Carolina Ferry System.

The shortest crossing is Cherry Branch to Minnesott Beach (2.3 miles, 20 minutes), and the longest crossing is Swan Quarter to Ocracoke Island (27 miles, 2 1/2 hours).

The shortest ferry is 125 feet long. The longest is 220 feet long.

North Carolina ferries operate in five different bodies of water - Pamlico Sound, Currituck Sound, Neuse River, Pamlico River and Cape Fear River.

Ferries operate at an average speed of 10 knots (about 8 miles per hour).

The ferries can operate in as little as five feet of water.

Sixteen ferries bear the school colors of the sixteen North Carolina state universities.

Every North Carolina ferry route is connected to a bicycling highway.

NOTE: Because the ferries to the outer banks are usually busy, it's a good idea to make a reservation in advance. There is also a charge to ride these ferries. All others are free.

For Reservations:

From Cedar Island to Ocracoke Island 1-800-856-0343 (toll free)
(Holds 50 cars, crossing takes 2 1/4 hours)

From Swan Quarter to Ocracoke Island 1-800-773-1094 (toll free)
(Holds 28 cars, crossing takes 2 1/2 hours)

One way fare for either Cedar Island or Swan Quarter:
Pedestrian $1.00, Bicycle $2.00, Motorcycles and cars or combinations less than 20' $10.00, Vehicles or combinations 20' to 40' $20.00, Vehicles or combinations not exceeding 55' $30.00

From Ocracoke to either Cedar Island or Swan Quarter 1-800-345-1665 (toll free)

For information:
Southport to Fort Fisher 1-800-368-8969 (toll free)
(Holds 38 cars, crossing takes 30 minutes)
One way fare: Pedestrian $.50, Bicycle $1.00, Motorcycles and cars or combinations less than 20' $3.00, Vehicles or combinations over 20' $6.00

Martin Vineyards

William "Billy" and Mary Lou Martin, David and Jeannie Martin
P. O. Box 186
Martin Farm Lane
Knotts Island, North Carolina 27950
(252) 429-3542 or (252) 429-3564

Opening Hours:
Monday - Saturday 10:00 a.m. to 6:00 p.m. & Sunday Noon - 6:00 p.m.

Billy Martin is a wrestler-farmer. No he doesn't wrestle the cows, or even the weather. He does have the usual tussles with weeds and pests, but with the Martin family of Knotts Island, wrestling and farming are so intertwined, it's difficult to separate one from the other.

Ever since he was a little boy, Billy Martin wanted to be a farmer. The fresh air and the joy of growing things appealed to him, even at a young age. His father was in the logging business near Aurora, North Carolina, and the boy grew up in the out of doors.

After World War II and college, Billy settled into a life of teaching Physical Education and coaching wrestling in Norfolk, Virginia. His coaching fame spread and he was named one of the top high school coaches in the nation, but Billy never lost his dream of farming. When he could afford it, he bought some land in the Virginia Beach area and started a small strawberry farm. It didn't stay small for long. The farm eventually grew to 150 acres and Billy was the largest grower in Virginia Beach.

His family grew too, seven children, three girls and four boys. With all the work that needs to be done on a family farm, the Martin children started early with farm chores. Everyone hoed strawberries, even little David.

"David always liked growing things, even as a little boy." says Billy. "All the kids would be hoeing strawberries and David would be sitting down on the ground at the edge of the row. They would say, 'Daddy, there he is. David's sitting down again.' I'd go over and I'd say, 'David, what are you doing, son?' and he'd say, 'I found a new plant here. What is it?' He was so fascinated with horticulture."

David, like his brothers, became a wrestler in high school. He was a four-time Virginia State Wrestling Champion, but, like his father, he never lost his love of growing things. He says that originally all the Martin children worked so hard on the farm that none of them wanted to be farmers, but eventually the draw was too much for David. He began working with Billy on the farm while his brothers worked with him in the wrestling business.

"I had more interest that anybody else in farming. I knew I didn't want to teach. I have one brother who teaches and coaches wrestling at Great Bridge High School in Chesapeake, Virginia, says David, where his son Michael, the next generation of Martin wrestlers and already a state junior champion, goes to school. The wrestling side of the family business produces video tapes and runs summer camps all over the country.

"Eventually development got too heavy at the Beach, so we moved down here. That was about 20 years ago. We found that the climate and the mineral soil were both perfect for growing grape vines and fruit trees. We're in the Fruitville Township of Knotts Island. It's a designated fruit region from the 1800's, so they've been growing fruit here for a long time." says David.

Knotts Island is surrounded by water, with the Atlantic Ocean and Knotts Island Bay to the east, and the Currituck Sound to the south and west. The Island is created by the canal on the north. This keeps it warmer in winter and cooler in summer. They have no frost problems, and only the occasional light snow. Although the sea breezes keep the area dry enough to need a lot of both drip and overhead irrigation, they also keep the moisture from setting in and causing mildew and rot. David says the growing conditions on Knotts Island are very California-like.

The Martin farm consists of 88 acres of peaches, apples, Scuppernong grapes and vinifera grapes. Everything is available for u-pick except the wine grapes. They also do a modest fresh fruit business to surrounding markets, and they make wine out of everything they grow. They are the only winery in the Carolinas located on the water.

"Growth in this area is at least a year faster than anywhere else," says David. "By the third year you generally get a full crop if the vine is ready. First you have to have a good healthy vine. Chardonnay is easy to grow. We begin harvesting it in late August. The Merlot is next and the Cabernet is our last grape coming in September." David grows all five of the Bordeaux varieties for his blends. Altogether there are 7.5 acres of vinifera. Two acres of vines are on their own root, protected from disease by the sandy soil. He is also growing Viognier, a popular grape in California that is making its way to the east coast.

When they made the move from Virginia Beach, David knew he wanted to grow vinifera wine grapes. Virginia Tech said it couldn't be done. "My dad thought I was nuts," laughs David, but he had a dream too. He wanted to make fine wines from grapes that he grew. A self-proclaimed self taught winemaker, David read everything he could and went to seminars and gatherings of wine-growers in Virginia and North Carolina. He started making wines to his taste, and found his customers liked them too.

David planted his first vines in 1987 and experimented for several years before opening the winery in 1996. He makes about 2000 cases of wine annually, but expects to increase volume as his newer vines start producing. He also makes wine from his apples and peaches, producing a delightfully light semi-dry cocktail wine from the latter.

Guests to Martin Vineyards can pick apples, peaches and Muscadines, and bring picnics to spread on tables down by the water. A large, open, grassy area is a great place for games and for kids to chase off some energy. Special events can be booked at Martin Vineyards. David says they've hosted several weddings, and he'd like to host a wine festival.

According to his dad, David still wrestles and can beat anybody, but these days he's most happy growing fruit and making wine. As for Billy, he lives in the old farmhouse and oversees the Martin family activities. The wrestler-farmer has the best of both worlds.

Directions
Take Highway 168 to the Currituck Sound Ferry. Ferry ride is free and takes 45 minutes. Follow State Road 615 to the where it swings north at the Methodist church (about 2 miles). Go straight, past the church, and stay on Woodleigh Road past the elementary school to Martin Farm Lane on your right.

Billy Martin (left) and David Martin on the front lawn of the 19th Century farmhouse that graces the labels of their wine bottles.

Wine List

Red Wines

Cabernet Sauvignon - a medium bodied wine with cherry and bell pepper flavors framed in toasty vanilla from ten month's American oak aging.

Merlot - a smooth wine with plum, mint and green olive flavors framed in oak.

Fruitville Red - a Bordeaux style blend of Cabernet, Merlot and Cabernet Franc. Flavors run from cherry to strawberry, ending with a chocolate/mint and vanilla finish.

White Wines

Chardonnay - lemon, apple and tropical fruit flavors. Barrel fermented in French and American oak to lend a buttery vanilla finish.

Semi-Dry White Wines

Muscadine - smells and tastes like the "Scuppernong" grape of the south. An old North Carolina tradition.

Bay Orchard Peach - plenty of peach flavors packed in this light golden sipper.

Bay Orchard Apple - a spicy blend of Gala, Golden Delicious and Granny Smith apples.

Fruitville White - a blend of Seyval and Chardonnay. A fruity picnic wine.

Sweet Blush Wines

Noble Blush (Red Muscadine) - a rosé style wine from the "Noble" Muscadine variety; a dark purple grape.

*Guests at Martin Vineyards are invited to bring
a picnic and enjoy the waterfront setting.*

While You're Here

The best way to see the Outer Banks is by boat. If you don't have your own, borrow one from the State of North Carolina and take the ferry. As the seagull flies, Knotts Island is about 15 minutes to the Atlantic Ocean and the sights of Corolla, but you'll have to take the u-drive route which takes over an hour from Currituck. Still, it is scenic and well worth it. History, nature and water sports make this a great vacation location.

Currituck County
Currituck to Knotts Island Ferry
The ferry crosses the Currituck Sound, carries 18 cars, and takes about 45 minutes. On a clear day you can see the Corolla Lighthouse, about 8 miles away. A great way to enjoy a picnic. Free

Departs Currituck	Departs Knotts Island
6:00 a.m.	7:00 a.m.
9:00 a.m.	10:00 a.m.
11:00 a.m.	Noon
1:00 p.m.	2:00 p.m.
3:30 p.m.	4:30 p.m.
5:30 p.m.	6:30 p.m.

Mackay Island National Wildlife Refuge
Knotts Island
8,646 acres located on the north side of Currituck Sound. Named for John

Mackie who owned the island in the early 1800's. Property purchased by Joseph Knapp in 1918. Knapp founded the organization Ducks Unlimited. Known for supporting significant migratory waterfowl populations. Boating, fishing, hiking and biking trails. Free
(252) 429-3100
Web site: www.fws.gov/~r4eao

Currituck Beach Lighthouse
Corner of NC 12 and Corolla Village Road, Corolla
First illuminated on December 1, 1875, this red brick tower is open for climbing. Keepers residence/museum. (Note: As the seagull flies, only six miles from Knotts Island. Humans in cars have to drive about 53 miles - well worth the trip).
Hours: April 1st to November 30th, 10:00 a.m. to 6:00 p.m. Daily
(252) 453-4939, Fax (252) 453-8152

Bed & Breakfast Inns in Corolla

The Inn at Corolla Light
1066 Ocean Trail
Corolla, NC 27927
(888) 546-6708 or (800) 215-0772 (toll free)
(252) 453-3340, Fax (252) 453-6927

Interesting Eats on Knotts Island

Knotts Island Cafe
Highway 615, North
Knotts Island, NC 27950
(252) 429-9600

Camden County
Dismal Swamp Wetlands and Boardwalk Project
"A Wetlands Learning Experience"
P. O. Box 858
Elizabeth City, NC 27909
A 639 acre parcel of land in the Great Dismal Swamp operated by Elizabeth City State University. On half mile boardwalk, observation tower, hiking, fishing.
Contact Dr. Maurice Powers, Office: (252) 335-3375 or (252) 335-3425
Home: (252) 336-4577 after 5:00 p.m.

Dismal Swamp Canal Welcome Center
Dismal Swamp National Wildlife
Refuge
2356 Hwy. 17 North
South Mills, NC 27976
Welcome center provides assistance
and information to both highway
and waterway travelers on historic
sites, attractions and other.
(252) 771-8333, Fax (252) 771-2055
(757) 986-3705 Refuge Information

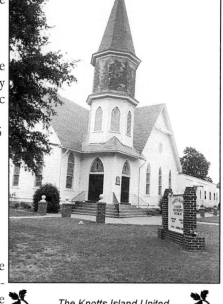

Pasquotank County
Elizabeth City
Museum of the Albemarle
1116 U. S. Highway 17 South
Elizabeth City, NC 27909
Galleries feature the story of the
people who have dwelled in the Albemarle region, from the Native
Americans to the first English-
speaking colonists, to the farmers
and fishermen who call the region

*The Knotts Island United
Methodist Church
is a local landmark.*

home. Regional branch of the North Carolina Museum of History. Free
(252) 335-1453, Fax (252) 335-0637

Historic Main Street District
502 E. Ehringhaus Street
Elizabeth City, NC 27909
Self guided tour of one of Elizabeth City's four National register Historic
Districts. Early 19th and 20th Century storefronts house specialty shop, restaurants, art galleries and antique shops.
(252) 335-4365, Fax (252) 335-0637 Chamber of Commerce

Bed & Breakfast Inns in Elizabeth City

The Culpepper Inn
609 W. Main Street
Elizabeth City, NC 27909
(252) 335-1993, Fax (252) 335-1555

Elizabeth City Bed & Breakfast
108 E. Fearing Street
Elizabeth City, NC 27909
(252) 338-2177, Fax (252) 338-5001

Guest House
600 West Main Street
Elizabeth City, NC 27909
(252) 331-2474
Fax (252) 331-2474

Dare County
Wright Brothers National Memorial
Hwy. 158, Kill Devil Hills
Site of the first powered air flight by Wilbur and Orville Wright. Museum, monuments, reconstructed hanger. Daily presentations.
(252) 441-7430

Bed & Breakfast Inns in Dare County

Advice 5 Cents - A Bed and Breakfast
111 Scarborough Lane
Duck, NC 27949
(800) 238-4235 (toll free), (252) 255-1050

3 Seasons Bed & Breakfast
4628 Seascape Drive
Kitty Hawk, NC 27949
(800) 847-3373 (toll free), (252) 261-4791

The Cherokee Inn
500 North Virginia Dare Trail
Kill Devil Hills, NC 27948
(800) 554-2764 toll free), (252) 441-6127, Fax (252) 441-1072
Web site: www.chaela.com/cherokeeinn

*A family picks
peaches at
Martin Vineyards.*

Bennett Vineyards

Buddy Harrell
6832 Bonnerton Road
Edward, North Carolina 27821

Mailing address
P. O. Box 150
Edward, North Carolina 27821

(800) 801-9725 (toll free), (252) 322-7154

Opening Hours: Monday - Saturday 2:00 to 5:00 p.m.

1996 was not a good year for Buddy Harrell. It should have been. The vines were well established and overflowing with grapes. The 1995 vintage of Bennett Vineyards wine was selling well in local shops and supermarkets, and all indications were that the 1996 harvest, less than a month away, would do even better. But Mother Nature had other plans.

On July 12th, the first of two disastrous hurricanes struck the North Carolina coast. As the crow flies, and the winds blow, Bennett Vineyards is only about a mile from the Pamlico Sound. The winds blew across the sound bringing with them rain and storm surge. Hurricane Bertha had barely finished toying with the state when Hurricane Fran roared on the scene with all the force she could muster. Buddy Harrell was left with broken vines, smashed grapes and a soggy vineyard. To add salt to the wound, he couldn't get any federal disaster relief because, at the time, he didn't live on the property. But that wasn't the end of it.

In November, Buddy's business partner, Bob Godley, died suddenly. Buddy was still reeling from the loss and deciding what to do next when he learned that Bob had not had clear title to the property on which the vineyard was located. Buddy had $30,000 worth of damaged vines on property he didn't own. But Buddy didn't give up.

While the property issue languished in probate, Buddy cleaned up the vineyard. He planted and replanted vines. He devised ideas to better market Bennett Vineyards. Though still recovering from Nature's battering, the vines netted 6,000 gallons of juice for 1997; not enough to supply the supermarkets, but enough to keep the operation going. Meanwhile, it began to look like getting title to the property was going to take years. Buddy decided to take a drastic step. He let the property go to auction.

"I was tired of not being able to do anything," he explains. "I couldn't sell anything, couldn't borrow any money 'cause I didn't have clear title. I talked it over with Farm Credit and I said, 'How about you foreclosing. I won't pay you and we'll put it up for public auction.' But they said 'You're liable to lose it if somebody bids on it,' and I said I'd have to take that chance."

In April, 1998 the property was auctioned off on the Beaufort County courthouse steps, and one man did bid against him. Farm Credit opened the bid at $52,000 to cover the debit and legal fees. Buddy started bidding.

"I said $53,000 and this other guy bid $60,000. So I said $60,001 and he said $62,000. Every time he'd bid, I'd go up a dollar. Finally he made one more bid, turned around and looked at me and walked off. He thought he was going to get it cheap, but I wasn't going to let it go."

Buddy's gamble paid off. He came away with clear title to the property and ready to get down to serious business.

The property had belonged to Bob Godley's mother. Through researching the family background, Bob had discovered that the sandy soil of what was formerly the Wiley T. Bennett Plantation had once been used to grow grapes for wine making. The idea was born and in 1991 Bob and Buddy planted 30 acres of Scuppernong (Carlos) and Muscadine (Noble) vines, with four acres of Nesbitt for the U-pick market.

It took a year and a half for the necessary permits to come through for the wine making side of the business. During that time, the vines grew and flourished. The partners adapted Buddy's father's old recipe for modern usage and made some test wines. In 1992, they did a survey with a "group of old timers, all over age 85, who were assembled to give an honest evaluation of the taste and fragrance of Bennett Vineyards wines." They were to compare the wines with the wines they remembered their fathers and grandfathers making, and some they themselves had probably made. The views of the panel were favorable and the partners produced their first saleable vintage of 200 gallons in 1993.

In 1994, production was up to 6,000 gallons. By 1995, they had secured a contract with a major supermarket chain to place Bennett Vineyards North Carolina Old Fashioned Homemade wines in 25 test stores. They produced 10,000 gallons that year. All was going great, then 1996 arrived.

"For two years I almost went broke. I thought about filing bankruptcy twice." says Buddy.

But he survived and now, with full ownership of the property and lots of ideas, he's ready to move Bennett Vineyards into the 21st Century. Plans are underway to build a new tasting room, a restaurant and a bed and breakfast. Lots of wildlife inhabit the area, including deer, and wild turkey, so he's thinking of creating a hunting lodge. Eventually he may utilize the beauty of Durham Creek which runs adjacent to the property, for a creek side wine room.

Bennett Vineyards is the largest commercial Muscadine vineyard in North Carolina.

For now, Buddy is concentrating on the products themselves. As the largest Muscadine vineyard in North Carolina, Bennett Vineyards has 31 acres in production, plus four acres of U-pick grapes. Plans are to plant another 35 acres within the next year. The U-pick business remains steady as does the fresh market sales to supermarkets in the southeast. Buddy says has had numerous requests to buy vines, so he is rooting vines to sell to the public. He recently started selling skins, seeds and stems to two pharmaceutical companies for the health and nutrition market. The most recent news out of California, says Buddy, is that grapevine prunings make a great charcoal flavoring for steaks, better than mesquite. Buddy can foresee in the near future every single part of the fruit and the vine having a marketable value. He says he'll be ready to sell.

Nobody said ever said growing a vineyard was easy. Buddy Harrell just didn't know it was going to be that hard. Hopefully, all the bad times are now behind him and with great ideas, hard work and excellent products, Bennett Vineyards will once again be "the best in the territory."

Directions

From Greenville, take State Road 33 east 40 miles to Edward. Go through town to NC Highway 1936 (a sign on the left side of the road points to the right). Turn right on NC Highway 1936 and go about 1 mile. Turn right at the sign into Bennett Vineyards and winery.

From New Bern, take State Road 55 east to Grantsboro. At Grantsboro, turn left onto Highway 306 and go north about 11 miles to where the highway joins State Road 33. Bear left and go about 1 or 2 miles to NC Highway 1936 and turn right (a sign on the right side of the road points to the left). Go about 1 mile and turn right at the sign into Bennett Vineyards and winery.

Wine List

North Carolina Old Fashioned Homemade Scuppernong Wine - a delicious, sweet white wine, made the old fashioned way. This wine is made by natural fermentation from selected and handpicked grapes so as to obtain a wine that smells like grape and tastes like grape. It is excellent for sipping before and after dinner. Serve chilled.

North Carolina Old Fashioned Homemade Muscadine Blush Wine - a delicious mixture of the white Scuppernong and black Muscadine grapes. Not quite as sweet as the white wine. An excellent quality wine to sip with the dinner meat. Serve chilled.

Bennett Vineyards wines are made from an 1840 recipe.

North Carolina Old Fashioned Homemade Muscadine Red Wine - a delicious red wine made from selected black Muscadine grapes. A nice, fresh Beaujolais style with good fruit. An excellent dinner wine. Serve chilled.

North Carolina Old Fashioned Homemade Colonial Scuppernong White Wine - a delicious white wine, dryer than our regular white wine.

North Carolina Old Fashioned Homemade Colonial Muscadine Red Wine - a delicious red wine, dryer than our regular red wine.

North Carolina Old Fashioned Homemade Cabaret Wine - a delicious red dry table wine.

North Carolina Old Fashioned Homemade Scuppernong Cider - a delicious sparkling cider made in the tradition of the early settlers. During the late 18th and early 19th Centuries, Scuppernong cider became know far and wide for its excellent and unusual taste. Our version is non-alcoholic, has no preservatives and no added sugar. It's sure to be a family favorite. Serve chilled.

North Carolina Old Fashioned Homemade Muscadine Classic Blush - non-alcoholic

While You're Here

After you leave Bennett Vineyards with your bottles of wine and freshly picked grapes, you might want to explore some of the history and towns of eastern North Carolina. Divided by the Pamlico River, Beaufort County was once the home of the notorious pirate, Blackbeard.

Beaufort County
Beaufort County Chamber of Commerce
102 Stewart Parkway
Washington, NC 27889
(252) 946-9168

Aurora Fossil Museum
4th & Main Streets, Aurora
PCS Phosphate, which has a huge mining operation in the area, sponsors the Aurora Fossil Museum. It's educational, fun, open all year round and admission is free.
(252) 322-4238

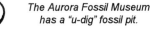

The Aurora Fossil Museum has a "u-dig" fossil pit.

Aurora to Bayview Ferry
From Aurora, head north on State Road 306 about 6 miles until you reach the ferry that crosses the Pamlico River. It runs year round, carries about 18 cars and the crossing takes about 30 minutes. Relax and watch the seagulls. Free
Departs Aurora

6:15 a.m.	12:45 p.m.
8:30 a.m.	2:15 p.m.
9:45 a.m.	4:45 p.m.
11:15 a.m.	6:15 p.m.
	8:30 p.m.
	10:00 p.m.
	12:30 a.m.

Belhaven

Belhaven Community Chamber of Commerce
P. O. Box 147
Belhaven, NC 27810
(252) 943-3770

Belhaven Memorial Museum
E. Main Street in City Hall
National Register of Historic Places. Free
(252) 943-6817

Bed & Breakfast Inns in Belhaven

Amble Inn B&B
242 Edward Street
Belhaven, NC 27810
(252) 943-3500

Belhaven Inn B&B
402 E. Main Street
Belhaven, NC 27810
(252) 943-6400

River Forest Manor
Country Inn & Restaurant
738 E. Main Street
Belhaven, NC 27810
(800) 346-2151 (toll free)
(252) 943-2151

The Duck Blind B&B
367 E. Water Street
Belhaven, NC 27810
(252) 943-6399

Interesting Eats in Belhaven

Farm Boys Restaurant
216 Pamlico Street
Belhaven, NC 27810
(252) 943-3295

The Helmsman Restaurant
238 Pamlico Street
Belhaven, NC 27810
(252) 943-3810

O'Neals Snack Bar
278 W. Main Street
Belhaven, NC 27810
(252) 943-6121

Mr. Pizza
271 Pamlico Street
Belhaven, NC 27810
(252) 943-3800

Bath

*Historic Bath
Visitor Center*
207 Carteret Street
Bath, NC 27808
(252) 923-3971
Founded in 1705, Bath is North Carolina's first town. Its most infamous resident was Edward Teach, better known as Blackbeard the Pirate. Restored homes and buildings from the 18th Century can be seen

The town of Bath has many historic houses and was once the home of Blackbeard the Pirate.

here as well as gift shops, a marina, and a peaceful harbor side park. Look for the Scuppernong vine in the garden of the Bonner House. After nearly 300 years, Bath remains a small village. Listed on the National Register of Historic Places.

Interesting Eats in Bath

Old Town Country Kitchen & Grill
436 Carteret Street
Bath, NC 27808
(252) 923-1840

Goose Creek State Park
Camp Leach Road, off State Road 92
1,596-acre natural area with 7.5 miles of nature trails, sandy swim beach and picnic area. 12 primitive campsites, wildlife-viewing opportunities and a boat ramp located on the Pamlico River. Free. Fee for camping.
(252) 923-2191, Fax (252) 923-0052

Washington

Washington Tourism Development Authority
102 Stewart Parkway
Washington, NC 27889
The original Washington, named for George before he became president.
(800) 999-3857 (toll free), (252) 946-9168, Fax (252) 946-9169

North Carolina Estuarium
223 E. Water Street
Washington, NC 27889
Focuses on the Albemarle-Pamlico estuarine system and on the Tar-Pamlico River.
(252) 948-0000

Partnership for the Sounds
P. O. Box 55, Columbia, NC 27925
The Partnership for the Sounds works to promote ecotourism on the Albemarle-Pamlico peninsula through a network of environmental education centers and opportunities. They produce a brochure and map featuring three self-drive tours. You may use the map alone or in conjunction with a one hour audio cassette. For information about the map and audio cassette, contact:
(888) 737-0437 (toll free), (252) 796-1000, Fax (252) 796-0218
Or in Washington, NC (252) 974-1044

Bed & Breakfast Inns in Washington

Acadian House Bed & Breakfast
129 Van Norden
Washington, NC 27889
(252) 975-3967, Fax (252) 975-1148

Pamlico House Bed & Breakfast
400 E. Main Street
Washington, NC 27889
National Register of Historic Places
(800) 948-8507 (toll free), (252) 946-7184, Fax (252) 946-9944
e-mail: pamlicohouse@coastalnet.com
Web site: www.bbonline.com/nc/pamlico

Pamlico County
Pamlico County Chamber of Commerce
P. O. Box 23
Bayboro, NC 28515
(252) 745-3008

Oriental
Oriental is know as the "Sailing Capital of North Carolina" and abounds with sailboats, sailing schools, charters and summer camps. Annual events

in this waterfront village of fewer than 1000 residents include the Running of the Dragon on New Year's Eve, the Croaker Festival on July 4th, the Tarpon Tournament in July, and the Oriental Cup Regatta in the fall. Lots of shops and galleries.

Bed & Breakfast Inns in Oriental

The Cartwright House
301 Freemason Street
Oriental, NC 28571
(888) 726-9389 (toll free), (252) 249-1337
e-mail: innkeeper@cartwrighthouse.com
Web site: www.cartwrighthouse.com (a great information site on Oriental)

The Inn at Oriental
508 Church Street/P. O. Box 726
Oriental, NC 28571
(800) 485-7174 (toll free), (252) 249-1078, Fax (252) 249-1201

Interesting Eats in Oriental

M & M's Cafe
205 S. Water Street
Oriental, NC 28571
(252) 249-2000

The Village Restaurant
Hwy. 55
Oriental, NC 28571
(252) 249-1700

The Oriental Marina Restaurant
Hodges Street/ P. O. Box 8
Oriental, NC 28571
(252) 249-2204

The Trawl Door
"at the foot of the bridge"
P. O. Box 166
Oriental, NC 28571
(252) 249-1232

Minnesott Beach to Cherry Branch Ferry
The ferry runs year round and takes you to the beaches of the Crystal Coast at Morehead City. The crossing takes about 20 minutes, holds about 30 cars and is free. The ferry departs Minnesott Beach every 20 minutes starting at 5:47 a.m. The last ferry departs at 1:15 a.m.

Craven County - New Bern
Craven County Convention & Visitors Bureau
314 Tryon Palace Drive/ P. O. Box 1413
New Bern, NC 28563
(800) 437-5767 (toll free), (252) 637-9400, Fax (252) 637-1919
e-mail: tourism@cravencounty.com

Founded in 1710 by Swiss and German immigrants, New Bern is North Carolina's second oldest town. Named for the Swiss capital, it boasts a restored waterfront historic district with shops and restaurants. A number of structures are on the National Register of Historic Places. "Bern" is the German word for bear, and the black bear symbol and statues can be found throughout the town. New Bern is the home of the state's first public school, the first printing press and newspaper, and the first official celebration of George Washington's birthday (yes, he slept here too). New Bern is also the birthplace of one of America's favorite soft drinks, Pepsi Cola.

Tryon Palace Historic Sites & Gardens
610 Pollock Street
North Carolina's first capitol and governor's mansion. Built in 1770, it has been completely restored. Daily tours of the palace and gardens also include the John Wright Stanly House visited by George Washington, the 1828 Dixon Stevenson House, the 1810 Robert Hay House, and the New Bern academy, one of the oldest secondary schools in America.
(800) 767-1560 (toll free), (252) 514-4900

Attmore-Oliver House & New Bern Historical Society
511 Broad Street Entrance at 510 Pollock Street
Historic 1790 home and grounds includes an 1884 brick smokehouse.
(252) 638-8558

Fireman's Museum
408 Hancock Street
One of the country's oldest fire companies still operating under its original charter. Museum has photographs and original fire fighting equipment.
(252) 636-4087

Bellair Plantation & Restoration
1100 Washington Post Road (just off Highway 43 north of New Bern)
The last and largest 18th Century brick plantation house in North Carolina. Long term restoration project begun in 1987 will return the house and grounds to their original glory.
(252) 637-3913

New Bern Trolley Tours
Narrated 90 minute tours of the historic district.
(252) 637-7316

Bank of the Arts
317 Middle Street
Craven Arts Council gallery exhibits works of regional, North Carolina and national artists in this restored 1912 bank building.
(252) 638-2577

Bed & Breakfast Inns in New Bern

Harmony House Inn
215 Pollock Street
New Bern, NC 28563
National Register of Historic Places
(800) 636-3113 (toll free), (252) 636-3810, Fax (252) 636-3810
e-mail: harmony@cconnect.net
Web site: www.harmonyhouseinn.com

Howard House Victorian Bed & Breakfast
207 Pollock Street
New Bern, NC 28563
(800) 705-5261 (toll free), (252) 514-6709, Fax (252) 514-6710
e-mail: howardhouse@coastalnet.com

Kings Arms Colonial Inn
212 Pollock Street
New Bern, NC 28563 *(cont. next page)*

National Register of Historic Places
(800) 872-9306 (toll free), (252) 638-4409, Fax (252) 638-2191
Web site: www.bbhost.com/kingsarmsinn

Magnolia House Bed & Breakfast
315 George Street
New Bern, NC 28563
(800) 601-9488 (toll free), (252) 633-9488, Fax (252) 633-9488

New Bern House Inn
709 Broad Street
New Bern, NC 28563
(800) 842-7688 (toll free), (252) 636-2250

Interesting Eats in New Bern

Fred & Claire's Restaurant
247 Craven Street
New Bern, NC 28563
(252) 638-5426

The Chelsea
335 Middle Street
New Bern, NC 28563
(252) 637-5469

Harvey Mansion Historic Inn
221 South Front Street
New Bern, NC 28563
(252) 638-3205

Sarah Pocket Tea Room
303 Metcalf Street
New Bern, NC 28563
(252) 636-3055

Sweet Bears Pastry Company
301 Middle Street
New Bern, NC 28563
(252) 635-5325

Trent River Coffee Company
208 Craven Street
New Bern, NC 28563
(252) 514-2030

Wine shops in New Bern

Wine Plus
3310 Trent Road
New Bern, NC 28563
(252) 635-5200

A Scuppernong vine grows in the garden
of an historic home in Bath.

"I love everything that is old:
old friends, old times, old manners,
old books, old wines."
- Oliver Goldsmith
She Stoops to Conquer

Duplin Wine Cellars

David and Ann Fussell
P. O. Box 756
Rose Hill, North Carolina 28458
(800) 774-9634 (toll free), (910) 289-3888, Fax (910) 289-3094

Opening Hours:
Monday - Saturday 9:00 a.m. to 5:00 p.m.
Closed New Year's Day, July 4th, Labor Day,
Thanksgiving Day & Christmas Day

Wine maker, grape grower, historian, museum curator, merchant, ad man and impresario; David Fussell is all of these and more. For a man who is supposed to be retired, he keeps awfully busy. David, along with his brother Dan, is co-owner of Duplin Wine Cellars in Rose Hill, North Carolina. At 85,000 gallons of wine annually, Duplin is North Carolina's second largest wine producer, and it's oldest.

In 1972, David was teaching school and Dan was building homes. Together they owned a small farm that they wanted to be more productive. At that time, Canandaigua Wines a large New York based wine consortium, was encouraging southern farmers to grow Muscadines for their wine production. Once the leading wine grape in America, Muscadines fell out of favor in the mid 20th century as European style wines became vogue. A return to Muscadine wines would mean profits for North Carolina growers. The brothers planted ten acres of vines. Soon Muscadine grapes were in plentiful supply, but with no contracts, local growers were forced to sell at low prices. This meant sell at a loss, or create an alternative. The Fussell brothers got creative.

"We didn't know a thing about making wine," says David, but it seemed the most appropriate thing to do with their wine grapes. "We went to Deerfield Vineyards (since closed) and Frank Williams and Charles Wood shared their knowledge of how to make wine. I also read everything I could get my hands on about wine making."

In 1975 they produced their first wines. David says, "They were drinkable."

1976 saw the brothers putting their lighthouse logo on the label and producing 3,500 gallons of wine from their ten acres of grapes. They sold every drop. At about the same time they realized they were going to need more grapes in order to produce more wine, several local farmers and business men decided that the wine business had potential. What began as a few investors and a cooperative of farmers is today a major company with 122 stockholders and 225 acres of Muscadine grapes.

In 1977, production leaped to 20,000 gallons. In 1978, it was 30,000 gallons and in 1979 it doubled to 60,000 gallons. They sold all of it.

By 1982, Duplin Wine Cellars' production was up to 120,000 gallons of wine and in 1983 it was 200,000 gallons. Like Garrett and Company, North Carolina's leading 19th century wine producer, there seemed to be no end to Duplin's ability to produce and sell wine, as long as the co-op continued to grow Muscadines to supply it. The brothers built a new production plant that was the most modern winery on the east coast. Then in 1984 they produced - 30,000 gallons of wine.

What happened was something that has plagued wine makers for over 100 years; government legislation. In late 1983, the Attorney General of North Carolina ruled that preferential laws that had been established by the state to promote grapes and wine making were unconstitutional. This meant that North Carolina wines could no longer be given preferred status in distribution. Sales dropped like rotting fruit.

"I thought that we could out work them," David relates. "But our sales dropped off so much that we had to sell off a lot of our equipment just to keep going." With no way to sell them, the growers stopped growing grapes. In 1986, Duplin Wine Cellars produced only 10,698 gallons. David says it has taken 15 years to get production and sales back up, and they still are less than half way to 1983's monumental year. In 1997, they made and sold 85,000 gallons.

"We are still limited to the amount of grapes we can acquire, says David. "We have access to 225 acres of grapes at the moment. We need 100 more acres. If we can get enough grapes to make the wine, I know we can sell it."

The resurgence of wine drinking in America as a whole has helped, but David says that there is something else that is once again pushing Muscadine wines to the forefront of the nation. Wine as medicine.

Recent studies point to the antioxidants in wines as being good for the heart. Ever the clever marketer, David Fussell seized on the idea and began selling wine making left-overs to pharmaceutical companies. After crush, the seeds, stems and skins are no longer needed for wines, but they contain a concentrated amount of an antioxidant called resveratrol. David says he not only sells the raw materials, but Duplin Wine Cellars has begun producing resveratrol as a medicinal tonic. Just 4 ounces per day will give you all the goodness of the grape you need. In addition, research at Campbell University has shown resveratrol in Duplin's Muscadine wines to be up to seven times higher than in European vintages.

"In the 1930's, there was a winery that operated in North Carolina that sold more wines to the pharmaceutical industry than it did to consumers as a beverage," says David. "That was the Parker Wine Company, and they marketed a feminine menstrual medicine. Today we know resveratrol is good for the heart. I would think that ten years from now, half of Duplin Wine Cellars' production will be for the pharmaceutical industry."

Wines, tonics, what else does Duplin Wine Cellars produce? We're glad you asked. A glimpse in the amply supplied wine shop reveals alcohol free Scuppernong wine jelly, a special recipe of resident chef John Ramariz, who also produces the menus and meals for Duplin's monthly dinner shows. April through December of each year, Duplin Wine Cellars hosts music, comedy, and special events in a banquet room that doubles as a wine history museum.

The museum contains artifacts from former North Carolina wineries, including an 18th century wine press, old photographs, tools and a fermenting tank from the Mother Vineyard. There are even bottles of 19th century wine including North Carolina's most famous wine, Virginia Dare. A 10 minute video of the history of wine making and Duplin Wine Cellars will tell you all you ever wanted to know and more. The museum is open to the public and individuals and groups are welcome.

Finally, a trip to Duplin Wine Cellars wouldn't be complete without a wine tasting at the oversized bar. Try a sip of each wine and take home the ones you like. Along with your bottles of wine you can purchase baskets, gift bags, corkscrews and other wine accessories. Don't forget your Duplin Wine Cellars logo wineglass, perfect for sipping a Scuppernong or contemplating a Carlos.

If you're lucky, you might get a few minutes with David Fussell. Ask him about North Carolina wines. He'll be glad to tell you. He's not only a wealth of information on wines, wineries and wine makers, he's added his own pages by helping to put Duplin Wine Cellars in the history books as well.

Directions
From Wilmington, take Interstate 40 north about 40 miles to Exit 380 to the town of Rose Hill. Turn right on U. S. Highway 117 and go north about seven blocks. The winery will be on your left.

Events at the Winery
Monthly dinner shows of music and comedy from April to December
Shows start at 7:00 p.m., $25.00 per person includes a selection of wines, dinner, and the show
Reservations are required - call (800) 774-9634 (toll free)

The Great Grape Stomp every September
Activities begin 10:00 a.m., Grape Stomp at 1:00 p.m.
Groups welcome, Bus parking and Handicap Accessible

"Duplin wine...
In moderation it's healthful.
In excess it's deadly.
In abstinence it's a crying shame."
- David Fussell, Winemaker
Duplin Wine Cellars, Inc.

Wine List

White Wines

Carlos - a dry wine which captures all the rich mellow characteristics of Vitis rotundifolia. Serve chilled with seafood and poultry.

Magnolia - a soft-dry, smooth and fruity wine with a fresh crisp finish. Magnolia's very name evokes the magic of the South. The juice of the Magnolia grape has a wonderfully balanced sugar-acid ratio. The balance is reflected n the wine. Serve chilled.

Scuppernong - the oldest and most famous variety of Vitis rotundifolia. No Southern plantation dinner would have been complete without this delicious dessert wine. Serve chilled.

Jonathan Murphy, Duplin Wine Cellars' Winery Manager, packs bottles into cartons for shipping to grocery stores.

Red Wines

Burgundy - the traditional Southern dry red wine. Great complexity can be achieved with careful bottle aging. The full-bodied dry wine is a perfect complement to red meat and cheese.

Rosé - quickly separating juice from red grape skins yields a wine with only a blush of color. A charming semi-dry wine for all occasions.

Hatteras Red - the traditional Southern red wine; slightly sweet and very fruity with a fresh crisp finish. This wine will bring back memories of the old South with its stately mansions, warm sunshine and gracious hospitality. Serve chilled.

Carolina Red - an old Southern recipe blends our Muscadines to produce this sweet red wine.

Scuppernong Blush - a smooth, fruity and sweet blush made from the famous Scuppernong, lightly blended with our Muscadine grape.

While You're Here

You're in plantation country here, lots of history and the first Spanish moss you'll see in North Carolina. Forty miles south on Interstate 40 will find you in Wilmington and the Cape Fear Beaches.

Cape Fear Coast Convention & Visitors Bureau
(800) 222-4757 (toll free), (910) 341-4030, Fax (910) 341-4029
e-mail: cape-fear.nc.us

Duplin County
Duplin County Tourism
P. O. Box 929
Kenansville, NC 28349
National Register Historic Districts are established in Wallace, Warsaw, Faison and Kenansville.
There are also museums in each of these town.
(800) 755-1755 (toll free), (910) 296-2180

World's Largest Frying Pan
Town Square, Rose Hill
Frying pan weighs 2 tons and is 15 feet in diameter.

Boney Mill Pond
Wallace
Built by John Boney, Jr. in the 1780's. Some of the original timbers still exist in the remains of the mill house.

Bed & Breakfast Inns in Duplin County

Country Squire's Restaurant & Squire's Vintage Inn
748 NC 24-50
Warsaw, NC 28398
(877) 830-1602 (toll free), (910) 296-1831, Fax: (910) 296-1431

Claddagh House, An Irish B&B Inn
210 Raleigh Road
Wallace, NC 28466
(910) 285-6144

McMillan Victorian Inn
109 Northwest Avenue
Teachey, NC 28464
(910) 285-5747

Kenansville

Liberty Hall Restoration
319 S. Main Street
Guided tour of the Kenan Plantation, c.1833. Eleven rooms and 12 out-buildings including garden shop, wine cellar, carriage house and servants quarters.
(910) 296-2175

Cowan Museum
411 S. Main Street
Over 2,000 items from household equipment to farming implements fill the historic Kelly-Farrior House that serves as a museum. Also on the grounds are a one-room school house, blacksmith shop and log cabin.
(910) 296-2149, Fax (910) 296-2107

Bed & Breakfast Inns in Kenansville

The Murray House
201 NC 24-50,
Kenansville, NC 28349
(800) 276-5322 (toll free), (910) 296-1000, Fax (910) 296-1000

Graham House B&B Inn
406 S. Main Street
Kenansville, NC 28349
(800) 767-9397 (toll free), (910) 296-1032

Among the over 2000 items at the Cowan Museum in Kenansville you'll find a furnished log cabin and a blacksmith shop.

North Carolina
The Heartland

Most works of art,
like most wines,
ought to be consumed
in the district
of their fabrication.
- Rebecca West (1892-1983), British author
Ending in Earnest,
"Journey's End Again" (1931)

David Fussell, Jr. of Duplin Wine Cellars assists two stompers at the North Carolina Grape Council's annual Grape Stomp held at the State Farmers' Market.

NC State Farmers' Market - Raleigh

(919) 733-7417, Fax (919) 733-9932

F ruits and vegetables, fresh baked breads, jams and jellies, garden plants - what could be more fun than a morning at the farmers' market! Raleigh is home to many state organizations, including the state Farmers' Market. The Market is open year round and offers shoppers and browsers a variety of North Carolina grown products. Among other North Carolina product vendors you'll find Ford's Fancy Fruits & Gourmet Foods who carry a large inventory of North Carolina wines from several wineries. Check out their web site as well as their catalog for wines and gift baskets.

The Farmers' Market has a large garden center, a restaurant (note the old buggies and wagons out front) and a large wholesale food terminal. It hosts activities throughout the year, including the North Carolina Grape Council's annual Grape Stomp each September.

Directions
Take the I-440 Outer Beltway south to Exit 297 (Lake Wheeler Road). Go north about two blocks and turn left into the Farmers' Market entrance.

Germanton Vineyard & Winery

David and Judy Simpson
Route 1, Box 1-G
Germanton, NC   27019
(336) 969-2075

Opening Hours:
Tuesday - Friday 10:00 a.m. to 7:00 p.m.
Saturday 9:00 a.m. to 5:00 p.m. Sunday 1:00 to 6:00 p.m.
Closed Monday

David Simpson didn't set out to own a winery. He wanted to paint, so owning an art gallery seemed a great way to pursue his interest and help other artists as well. At the same time he started work on his dream gallery, he and wife Judy bought an interest in the local vineyard owned and operated by friend Bill McGee. Bill saw grapes as an alternative to growing tobacco long before other farmers started looking for new crops. He gathered several friends who were interested in the idea, and they invested money as well as time. Everyone contributed, but when Bill died suddenly, the vineyard was in danger of closing. Of all the investors, David was the most likely one to take over the wine business, so in 1981, he opened the first art gallery-winery in the country.

Today, Germanton Vineyards & Winery produces five wines from 23 acres of Seyval Blanc, Niagara and Chambourcin grapes scattered around the historic village of Germanton. That's about 3000 gallons annually. Blended wines include grapes from a nearby vineyard, but all of the grapes are grown in the North Carolina Piedmont and handled expertly by wine master Jerry Pegram. The work is done by hand, and all of the wines are made from pure juice with no water added. David says they sell out of everything each year.

Germanton Gallery represents more than 80 artists from all over the world, hosts workshops and gala exhibitions and has been the starting point for numerous national art tours. Both the gallery and the winery operate compatibly out of a luxuriously renovated 1920's vintage gas station and garage in the tiny Piedmont town of 200.

"If you create what people want, and you create a destination for them, they will come." says David of his seemingly "off the beaten path" location. "People love beautiful things and wine and art go together. After all, wine is liquid art."

Taking the idea a step further, David has on occasion commissioned artists to paint pictures for the labels on the wine bottles. In conjunction with American Farmland Trust (AFT), he commissioned nationally known artist David Armstrong to paint a pastoral scene that graces his "Dogwood White" Seyval wine. A portion of the proceeds from the sale of this wine goes to AFT to help protect America's agricultural resources.

The regular bottle labels are also works of art, depicting water color scenes by Jerry Dillingham of sunny vineyards and succulent bunches of grapes. The Seyval, the Vermillion and the Sweet White are all award winners, the first two having taken a silver and a bronze medal at the Dixie Classic Fair in Winston-Salem, and the Sweet white winning a bronze medal at the Eastern Wine Competition in Rochester, New York.

The gallery houses two floors of original art, prints, antique maps and documents from North and South Carolina dating from the Civil War. Works in water color, acrylics and oils, nature scenes, still lifes, portraits, western art, modern art - all are represented. Prices start around $15 for original prints. Custom framing is also available.

The tasting room occupies the front corner of the ground floor, with a 12 foot long oak bar gracing the ancient brickwork. More paintings decorate the walls behind the bar as well as framed medals and award certificates. An 8 1/2 x 11 inch black and white sign sets the mood by declaring "We won't sell unless you're sufficiently aged."

"It's fun." David says. "We want to have fun with what we're doing here. Life is too short to do otherwise."

Directions to Germanton Vineyards & Winery

From Winston-Salem, go north on U. S. Highway 52 to Highway 8 North. Take Highway 8 north 7 1/2 miles to Germanton. As you come into town, the winery is on your left.

Wine List

Seyval Blanc - an excellent dry, white table wine made entirely from the Seyval Blanc grape, this wine is Germanton's answer to Chablis. It has an excellent aroma and a clean, smooth taste to be enjoyed for all occasions. Serve chilled.

Autumn Blush - a delightfully pleasant medium dry wine blended from hand-picked select grapes, harvested at the peak of their maturity. This wine may be served as a cocktail and will compliment many seafood or chicken menus. It is Germanton's answer to White Zinfandel, Serve chilled.

Vermillion - an outstanding red dinner wine fermented and aged to complete dryness. The rich, red color and a slight aroma of oak makes this well-balanced wine a delightful companion with beef. It is Germanton's answer to Cabernet Sauvignon. Serve at room temperature.

Sweet Red Wine - a smooth, sweet country red wine made completely from the juice of the grape. It is best enjoyed before or after dinner. Serve slightly chilled.

Sweet White Wine - a fruity, sweet white wine that tastes and smells like a walk through the vineyard at harvest time. Enjoy before or after dinner. Serve chilled.

David Armstrong "Dogwood White" - a special edition Seyval wine with a label depicting a watercolor painting by nationally-known artist David Armstrong. David's work reveals an overwhelming concern for the beauty of the earth and all that still can be preserved, as do the fine wines produced by Germanton Winery. A portion of the proceeds are donated to the American Farmland Trust, the nation's only non-profit, membership organization dedicated to protecting our valuable agricultural resources.

*Paintings and wines
are the featured arts
at Germanton
Vineyard & Winery.*

Hanging Rock State Park features hiking, picnic areas and scenic beauty.

While You're Here

North Carolina's premier state park is located just north of Germanton, and it's newest historic site is just 18 miles to the east. The area is great for picnics and outdoor activities. Not only are you in an historic and scenic part of the state, you're a stone's throw from shopping, restaurants and museums in Winston-Salem, so plan to spend a few days.

Hanging Rock State Park
In the ancient Sauratown Mountains. Park has five waterfalls, a cave, three ridge tops and over 18 miles of hiking trails; also camping and cabins. Free
(336) 593-8480, Fax (336) 593-9166

Old Mill of Guilford
1340 Hwy. 68 N., Oak Ridge
A 200 year old water-powered operating gristmill. Free
(336) 643-4783

Pinnacle & Pilot Mountain
Pilot Mountain State Park
U. S. Highway 52/Rt. 3, Box 21
Pinnacle, NC 27043

Horn Creek State Historic Site is the former home of the Hauser family and is a working early 20th Century farm.

Divided into two sections, with 1,000 acres located on Hauser Road on the Yadkin River. Hiking trails, scenic overlooks, picnicking, family and group camping and climbing area. Steep, mountain road to the top of mountain but well worth the climb. Free.
(336) 325-2355, Fax (336) 325-2751
email: pilotmtn@ols.net

Horne Creek Living Historical Farm State Historic Site
320 Hauser Road
Pinnacle, NC 27043
Restoration of the former Hauser Family Farm, depicts rural life in North Carolina's northwest Piedmont around 1900 to 1910. House, out-buildings, crops, living history. (Note: Follow the signs off U. S. Highway 52. You go a "fur piece" down the road to get there so don't give up. Near the entrance to the Yadkin River section of Pilot Mountain State Park.)
(336) 325-2298, Fax (336) 325-3150
e-mail: hornecreek@ncsl.dcr.state.nc.us

Bed & Breakfast Inns in Pilot Mountain

Blue Fawn Bed & Breakfast
3052 Siloam Road/P. O. Box 986
Pilot Mountain, NC 27041
(800) 948-7716 (toll free), (336) 374-2064

Scenic Overlook Bed & Breakfast
Scenic Overlook Lane/P. O. Box 490
Pilot Mountain, NC 27041
(336) 368-9591, Fax (336) 368-1342
e-mail: scenic@idt.net
Web site: www.bbonline.com/nc/scenic

Flippins Bed & Breakfast
203 W. Main Street
Pilot Mountain, NC 27041
(336) 368-1183

Danbury
Moratock Park
Sheppard Mill Road
Located on the Dan River, includes the Ironworks National Historic Site, one of the best preserved iron smelting furnaces known to exist in North Carolina. Built around 1843. Picnicking, swimming, tubing and canoeing.

Bed & Breakfast Inns in the Area

MeadowHaven B&B Vacation Rentals
State Road 8
Germanton, NC 27019
(336) 593-3996

Trails Inn
129 Sante Fe Trail
Pinnacle, NC 27043
(336) 325-3268

"I think of wine as liquid art."
- David Simpson
Germanton Vineyard & Winery

Westbend Vineyards

Jack and Lillian Kroustalis
5394 Williams Road
Lewisville, North Carolina 27023
(336) 945-5032

Opening Hours:
Friday & Saturday 12:00 to 6:00 p.m.
Sunday 1:00 to 6:00 p.m.

When Jack and Lillian Kroustalis bought the old tobacco farm in 1972, they had no idea that Jack's hobby vineyard would one day be one of the top wine producing vineyards in the Southeast. Jack's hobby just got out of hand.

"Jack had an interest in growing things," says Lillian, who is the epitome of the gracious southern lady. "He was particularly interested in growing a vineyard. He planted some blueberries, some pears and peaches, but what he really wanted to grow was French varietals; Vitis vinifera."

The only vineyard experimenting with growing vinifera in North Carolina at the time was Biltmore Estate Winery. All the experts said it couldn't be done, but that didn't deter Jack. He and Lillian planted two acres of "some of everything" in 1973. "It was our experimental plot," says Lillian. The vines flourished in the rich soil of the Yadkin River valley. Soon they planted more vines and the grape harvests got bigger. By 1986 Jack and Lillian had 30 acres in vines and a 70-ton grape harvest that was being sold to other wineries. The next question was a logical one. Why not open a winery and use the grapes themselves? So, that's just what they did.

In 1988, Jack and Lillian built a small 2000-case production facility and Westbend became a bonded winery. The name Westbend refers to the nearby area where the Yadkin River takes a bend to the west before continuing its southern journey. They hired oenologist Steve Sheppard in 1989 to be wine maker and general manger for the new operation. Steve had been the wine maker at two Pennsylvania wineries.

In 1990 Westbend Vineyards released its first wines, 1988 and 1989 vintages. "We knew when people tasted it, they would recognize it as a quality wine." says Lillian. They began marketing their wines, then the best thing happened. At a wine competition in Watkins Glen, New York, their Barrel Fermented Chardonnay won a gold medal and the Kendall Jackson took the silver. "That made a loud noise and we used it as much as we could. After that, it got easier."

Today, those original two acres that Jack and Lillian planted are mature vines, producing marvelous grapes after more than 25 years. Added acreage has brought the vineyard up to 45 acres. "We've had success without any major problems," says Lillian. "We found that you can grow high quality Vitis vinifera in the Piedmont and the foothills." At an elevation of 950 feet, they have the right climate and generally get just enough snow to keep the ground cold without being harsh. This keeps the vines from budding too early. Their only major problem each year is the possibility of late spring frosts. A huge wine machine in the middle of the vineyard is their only insurance against crop loss if that happens.

Westbend is a commercial winery, producing about 10,000 cases annually of award winning wine. A number of medals over the years have established Westbend as one of the south's premier wineries. Robert Parker of "The Wine Advocate" has called Westbend "One of the South's best kept secrets' and declared that, "As fine as their wines are, I am surprised they are not better known outside of North Carolina."

Visitors to the winery can take a winery tour, taste the wines in the tasting room and browse the wine shop. Tables with umbrellas invite lounging and sipping and you are encouraged to bring picnics. There is even a grill for cooking and large outdoor fireplace keeps the patio cozy even on chilly days or evenings. The large tasting room is available for private parties and tastings, but because they are a year-round working winery and the visitor area is small, there are no special events scheduled. Lillian says if you arrive at harvest time, you could be put to work.

"Westbend wines are estate produced and bottled." Lillian explains. They would like to increase production and are looking at planting more acreage. Some hobbies just don't end.

Directions
Go 15 miles west of Winston-Salem on Highway 421 North. Take the Shallowford Road exit and turn left. Go 2 miles and turn left onto Williams Road. Entrance to the vineyards is the first paved road on the left

Guests can picnic among the vines at Westbend Vineyards.

Wine List

Barrel Fermented Chardonnay - elegant and intense with lots of spicy oak aromas. Silky texture with toasty honey and butterscotch rounding out the finish.

Chardonnay - French oak aged dry white wine vinted in the style of a white Burgundy. Appley- pear nose with a hint of citrus. Serve chilled with seafood, veal or fowl.

Seyval Blanc - a French derived grape, soft on the palate. This fresh, fruity medium dry wine will accompany most any entree.

Riesling - Clean, fresh, light semi-dry white wine. Lovely nose of perfume, spice and honey notes the Germanic style. Serve chilled with lighter foods.

Sauvignon Blanc - dry white with ripe aromas and flavors of fruit and grass, slightly woody, crisp acidity with a long clean finish.

White Gamay - rich, spicy medium dry rosé wine produced from the Gamay grape of Beaujolais. Its style permits the wine to be served with a wide spectrum of foods.

Muscat Canelli - a delicious white varietal, brilliantly spicy, fruity and plentiful. Its lightly sweet elegance combines with honey, grapefruit and peach flavors which finishes rich and clean. A beautifully balanced wine.

Vidal Blanc - amber gold with honey, toasted almond and orange blossom aromas. Intensely concentrated with apricot, peach and caramel-apple flavors that linger on and on.

Premium Red Varietals

Cabernet Sauvignon - concentrated with rich dark chocolate and herbal currant flavors. Balanced with a solid backbone of acid and soft tannins.

Chambourcin - this fruity, dry red wine will accompany pasta, lamb, red meat and spicy foods. Similar to a red Burgundy.

Merlot - deep berry floral and tobacco accents up front. Solid cherry and plum flavors combine in this rich varietal dry red wine.

Pinot Noir - bright cherry color with intriguing aromas of raspberry, bacon and leather. The firm acidity structures an earthy complex core of fruit, oak, vanilla and soft tannins.

While You're Here

The Winston-Salem area has much to offer visitors. State parks, historical sites, shopping, galleries, it's all here, so plan to spend a few days. Be sure to buy some Moravian cookies at the Old Salem bakery. They're baked in the original brick oven and are delicious with a glass of Westbend Riesling.

Winston-Salem Convention & Visitors Bureau
601 West 4th Street/P. O. Box 1409
Winston-Salem, NC 27102
(800) 331-7018 (toll free), (336) 728-4200, Fax (336) 721-2202
e-mail: bmccoy@winstonsalem.com

Old Salem
Old Salem Road at Academy Street
Founded in 1766 as a Moravian congregational town, Old Salem is one of America's most authentic and well-documented colonial sites. Costumed interpreters recreate late 18th Century and early 19th Century life in this living history town. Daily demonstrations. Winkler bakery, tavern restaurant, shops, museum and gallery.
(888) 348-5422 (toll free), (336) 721-7300, Fax (336) 721-7335

The Single Brothers Workshop (c. 1771) is one of the many preserved and restored buildings you'll find in Old Salem.

Diggs Gallery
Winston-Salem State University
601 Martin Luther King, Jr. Drive
Winston-Salem, NC 27110
Rotating exhibits spotlight Winston-Salem's rich African-American heritage. 6,500 square feet of gallery space. Educational programs offered.
(336) 750-2458

Museum of Anthropology
Wingate Road at Wake Forest University/P. O. Box 7267
Winston-Salem, NC 27109
Exhibit consists of objects from the Americas, Africa, Asia and Ocenia. Household and ceremonial items, textiles, hunting and fishing gear, and objects of personal adornment are presented thematically.
(336) 758-5282, Fax (336) 758-5116
e-mail: berman@wfu.edu

Museum of Early Southern Decorative Arts (MESDA)
924 S. Main Street in Old Salem
The only museum dedicated to exhibiting and researching regional decorative arts of the Early South. Guided tour of 21 exhibit rooms and six galleries.
(888) 348-5422 (toll free), (336) 721-7300, Fax (336) 721-7335
e-mail: visit@oldsalem.org

Reynolda House, Museum of American Art
2250 Reynolda Road
Magnificent former home of Katharine Smith and Richard Joshua Reynolds, founder of R. J. Reynolds Tobacco Company. Visitors will enjoy the extraordinary collection of 18th , 19th and 20th Century American paintings and sculpture.
(336) 725-5325, Fax (336) 721-0991
e-mail: reynolda@ols.net

Southeastern Center for Contemporary Art (SECCA)
Across from Reynolda House
Series of cascading galleries housed in the 1929 English style home of the late industrialist, James G. Hanes. Rotating guest exhibits.
(336) 725-1904

Historic Bethabara Park
2147 Bethabara Road
Site of 1753 Moravian Village with 190 acre park and 1788 Gemeinhaus (church). Where the Moravians first settled before founding Old Salem.
(336) 924-8191, Fax (336) 924-0535

SciWorks
400 W. Hanes Mill Road
Science Center and Environmental Park of Forsyth County offers interactive exhibits, planetarium and 15 acre park with otter habitats and farm animals.
(336) 767-6730, Fax (336) 661-1777

Bed & Breakfast Inns in Winston-Salem

Augustus T. Zevely Inn
803 S. Main Street (Old Salem)
Winston-Salem, NC 27101
National Register of Historic Places
(800) 928-9299 (toll free), (336) 748-9299, Fax (336) 721-2211

Henry F. Shaffner House
150 S. Marshall Street
Winston-Salem, NC 27101
(800) 952-2256 (toll free), (336) 777-0052, Fax (336) 777-1188

Lady Anne's Victorian Bed & Breakfast
612 Summit Street
Winston-Salem, NC 27101
National Register of Historic Places
(336) 724-1074
Web site: www.bbonline.com/nc/ladyannes

Interesting Eats in Winston-Salem

Old Salem Tavern and Dining Room
Old Salem
(336) 721-7300

Mayberry Restaurant
Old Salem
(336) 721-7300

The Summerhouse and Arbor (c.1754, 1758) appears on the first map of Bethabara, the original Moravian settlement in the area. The Moravians planted vines to make wine for their use and for export to Pennsylvania.

The Horse's Mouth Coffeehouse
424 W. Fourth Street
Winston-Salem, NC 27101
(336) 773-1311

Waldo's Wings
3616 Reynolda Road
Winston-Salem, NC 27106
(888) 283-0511 (toll free), (336) 924-9232

Ted's Kickin' Chicken
6973 Yadkinville Road
Pfafftown, North Carolina
(336) 945-0299

Dennis Vineyards

Pritchard and Lynda Dennis
24043 Endy Road
Albemarle, North Carolina 28001
(704) 982-6090

Opening Hours: By appointment

Pritchard Dennis should not be growing grapes. He shouldn't even be alive, but by the grace of God and the skilled hands of a gifted neurosurgeon, Pritchard has outlived his three week prognosis long enough to plant vines and start making wine.

In 1985, Pritchard owned and operated a small brick plant near his home in Albemarle. While trying to repair a beam in the plant, he fell, tearing an artery at the stem of his brain. At that time, his condition was considered inoperable and Pritchard was told to get his affairs in order. Doctors could only give him three weeks to live.

However, through the efforts of his local doctor, Pritchard's condition was made known to Charlotte neurosurgeon, Dr. Larry Rogers, who pioneered arterial bypass surgery for aneurysm. Dr. Rogers agreed to operate, and after one 12 hour surgery and a second 4 hour surgery to clear clotting, Pritchard became the first patient to survive the procedure.

Following the operations, Pritchard was paralyzed and totally blind. He could only hear what was going on around him and feel the respirator moving his chest. As the weeks rolled by, he began to move one finger, then two, gradually recovering his speech, half of his sight and most of his movement. One year later he could walk again.

"A year after the surgery, Dr. Rogers and I were saying our good-byes. I had a list of stuff that didn't work that I wanted to ask him about." says Pritchard. "He'd originally told me not to ask about prognosis, but today I said now I'm going to ask you. Well, he said 'we think we can give you five years, maybe even ten years.' I said that's great, I'll try to use them well."

And use them he did, living day by day. There were times when he could control his disabilities and times when they controlled him. A deficiency of oxygen to the brain meant he could live at an elevation no higher than 1000 feet above sea level. Since his home in the North Carolina Piedmont is at just about that height, Pritchard couldn't survive the thinner air of the area for very long. He and Lynda moved to the coast, spending only a few months each year in Albemarle.

As part of his physical therapy, Pritchard started shrimping. "They wanted me to get my heart rate up so far and hold it there." he says. "Shrimping seemed a good way to do that. I'd shrimp by myself. The family would raise Cain about it, but I could take the shrimp boat and work myself just as hard as I needed to work myself and enjoy it. So I worked. Then a buddy and I got more serious about it and we started shrimping the ocean. One morning we caught 550 pounds of shrimp. We also used to black bass fish a lot. We had a spot off shore where there were acres of fish. We used electric reels and just wenched them up as fast as we could."

Besides telling fishing stories, during this time, Pritchard also started studying wine making. "You see, wine making is in my ancestry. My grandfather tried to teach me how to make wine, although his came out bad half the time. I started reading all the old masters, everything I could get my hands on. I have textbooks from all the leading viticulture schools in the country and I figured out what Grampa was doing wrong."

He was also making wine during this period, perfecting techniques and blends. Six years after he started his study, he decided to go from hobbyist to professional. His health continued to improve, so he and Lynda were able to return to Albemarle year round. The 10th year passed. In the 11th year, Pritchard Dennis planted a vineyard.

"A lot of people thought I was crazy planting a vineyard, but I figured the Lord got me this far, he'd see me through." laughs Pritchard. "Sixteen months after I planted the first vines, I had grapes. Then the vision in my right eye started to come back. There is no medical reason for that eye to be working again. I wore a patch over it for 12 years, but now it's working again. I figure the Lord said, 'I'm going to give that guy all those grapes down there, he needs both eyes. I'm going to start that eye back up.'"

Not only is Pritchard Dennis a miracle man in the world of medicine, it appears he is one in the world of grape growing as well. The usual time frame from planting to yield is two to three years. Pritchard's vines produced wine-ready grapes in 16 months. Muscadine vines produce in clusters, averaging 15 grapes to a cluster. Pritchard's vines are producing clusters of 20 to 60 grapes. Naturally, the state viticulture researchers want to know how he does it so Dennis Vineyards is also a research station for Muscadines. He works closely with the North Carolina Agriculture Department.

"The flavor is generated in the vineyard." Pritchard says. "We grow all of our own grapes. Nobody grows grapes like I want them grown. During the growing season, you'll find me in the vineyard tasting the grapes waiting for that flavor to get there. I check 50 places in the vineyard and several grapes at each place. People say, 'What'd you have for lunch?' I say, 'Grapes!' This goes on for two months out of the year." Which may be one reason Pritchard says that his normally high cholesterol count has dropped over the past year. "I eat a lot of grapes and I drink a lot of wine." he says.

Pritchard primarily grows Carlos and Noble. He also grows Ison, a patented vine he buys from the inventors in Georgia. His wines include the varietals as well as blends. They are light and are of varying degrees of dryness.

Dry Muscadine wine?

"I'm a dry wine drinker and I'm a wine maker, so that makes me altogether different. My taste buds are tuned to what I want it to come to after fermentation - no sugar - bone dry." Pritchard explains. "Sugar is an enemy to me. I don't even give the yeast all the sugar to begin with. I give it just enough for it do what I want it to do."

Which is what makes Dennis Vineyards wines unique in the world of Muscadine.

"The Carnola reminds me of Spanish table wine." Pritchard explains. "When you go to a restaurant in Madrid, they bring you a pitcher of wine. That was what I had in the back of my mind when I started to generate my wine. My idea was to have wines that I could set out, and whether you were a wine drinker, a non-wine drinker, a vinifera wine drinker - if you drink strictly Beaujolais or Cabernet Sauvignon - I'd have something that, if you wanted to drink Muscadine wine, you could like."

Dennis Vineyards is the new kid on the North Carolina wine grower's block, producing it's first vintage in 1997. It is a family affair. Both Dennis sons help with the business, although Pritchard says his youngest son Sandon is most interested in the wine making process. He and Pritchard work together to make Dennis Vineyards wines. Eventually he will take over the wine making altogether.

"I'm a man living on borrowed time," says Pritchard. "Every day, I cherish, and I love my work. I work 24 hours a day." He leans back in his chair. " Right now - I'm aging my wine."

Directions
About 40 miles east of Charlotte. From Albemarle, take state road 24/27 west for about 5 miles to the Endy caution light. Turn right on Endy Road. Go past the school to the 4th house on the left. Please call for appointment before you arrive.

All of the Dennis family help in the business. Pritchard's grandchildren, Hannah and Nathan, work in the vineyard after school planting and tending the vines.

Wine List

Carlos - a light dry white wine

Noble - a full bodied, semi-dry red that goes well with red meats

Ison - a dry red table wine with complex characteristics

Carnola Red Table Wine - a sweet red wine that is a blend of Carlos and Noble

Carnola Semi-Dry Table Wine - a red wine with a light touch of sugar from a unique blend of Carols and Noble

Carnola Dry Table Wine - a light dry red table wine that is a blend of Carlos and Noble

While You're Here

There's a slight roll to the land, enough to tell you you're in the Piedmont. With both Charlotte and the Uwharrie National Forest nearby, you can go from city slick to back woods primitive all in one day, so pack your car for every event.

Charlotte Convention & Visitors Bureau
122 E. Stonewall
Charlotte, NC 28202
(704) 334-2282, Fax (704) 342-3972

Info Charlotte
330 S. Tryon
Charlotte, NC 28202
(800) 231-4636 (toll free)

Stanly County
Morrow Mountain State Park
49104 Morrow Mountain Road
Albemarle, NC 28001
A 4,693 acre natural resource area located in the ancient Uwharrie Mountains. Overnight camping, hiking, picnicking, boating, fishing, pool swimming and vacation cabins.
(704) 982-4402, Fax (704) 982-5323

Stanly County Museum
245 E. Main Street
Albemarle, NC 28001
History of Stanly County. Includes tours of two local historic houses.
(704) 986-3777, Fax (704) 986-3778

Reed Gold Mine State Historic Site
9621 Reedmine Road
Stanfield, NC 28163
Site of America's first gold discovery (a 17 pound nugget). Museum, orientation film, guided underground tour, a Stamp Mill and walking trails.
(704) 721-4653, Fax (704) 721-4657
e-mail: reedmine@aol.com

Montgomery County

Uwharrie National Forest
50,189 acres of wilderness. Camping, boating, bridle trails, fishing, hiking trails, picnicking and swimming.
(910) 576-6391

Town Creek Indian Mound State Historic Site
509 Town Creek Mound Road
Mount Gilead, NC 27306
Reconstructed ceremonial center includes the major temple on an earthen mound. Visitor center, slide presentation and nature trail.
(910) 439-6802, Fax (910) 439-6802
e-mail: tcim@ac.net

Bed & Breakfast Inns in Montgomery County

The Pines Plantation Inn LLC.
1570 Lilly's Bridge Road
Mount Gilead, NC 27306
(800) 711-1134 (toll free), (910) 439-1894, Fax (910) 439-1894
e-mail: pinesinn@aol.com
Web site: www.bbonline.com/nc/pinesinn

Gold Hill

Village of Gold Hill
St. Stephen's Church Road, Off U. S. Highway 52
Richest mining property east of the Mississippi River. Home of America's first gold rush. Gold Hills Mines Historic Park contains three gold mines, rock jail and Mauney's 1840 Store.
Web site: www.salisbury.net/goldhill

Tiny clusters of grapes begin to form on the vines in late May and early June.

North Carolina Waldensian Products

Eunice Bumgarner and Chris Cook
1530 19th Street SW
Hickory, North Carolina 28602
(828) 327-3867, Fax (828) 327-8279

Tasting Counter Hours: Thursday - Saturday 10:00 a.m. to 6:00 p.m.
Tasting counter located at Hickory Furniture Mart, 2220 Hwy. 70 SE

Once upon a time, three friends decided to reopen a winery that had been closed for many years. They pooled their resources, got the wine and started selling it. Straight forward. End of story, right? So why is Eunice Bumgarner selling wine at the Hickory Furniture Mart?

Well, it's it little round about here. The Bernard winery was originally opened in 1935 by Mellie C. Bernard who produced Waldensian style wines from old family recipes. The Waldensians were French speaking Protestants from the Italian Alps who settled in Burke County at the end of the 19th Century. The Bernard winery took a twist on the wines made in the old way by making use of the native grapes that grow so abundantly in the region. For 13 years, the wines and the winery were popular. Then, in 1948, Bernard was forced to close down when Burke County went dry.

The winery and its equipment sat for over 30 years and a number of people thought that was a shame.

Then in the early 1980's Bernard's son Mellie J. Bernard, Leonard Bumgarner and Lorin Weaver started discussing the idea of reopening the old winery. With the old equipment still there, they were sure they could make it work. However, the reality was just that - work, and a lot of it - and the three decided that making the wine was going to take more time than any of them had. Mellie still had his father's old wine recipes. David Fussell of Duplin Wine Cellars agreed to make the wine and the partners would distribute it. Thus began the North Carolina Waldensian Winery.

The venture soon proved to be too time consuming for Mellie, so he sold his part of the business to Leonard and Lorin. That worked for a while, but then Lorin too, decided that he was no longer able to continue, leaving Leonard as the sole owner. That was fine with him. Leonard was a salesman and he loved people. He was also interested in wine and wanted to build up a route and deliver the wine himself. It gave him an opportunity to do what he loved best, travel and talk to people. For two years Leonard distributed his wine to places around the state, but failing health soon had him hiring someone else to drive the truck. As his health deteriorated, his wife Eunice became more involved as did son-in-law Chris Cook. Leonard's one wish was that she somehow keep the business going.

Leonard died in December 1996 after a long illness. Suddenly, Eunice had a wine distribution business on her hands.

"When Leonard got to where he wasn't able to - somebody, you know - you get into this and you got to keep it going. You do what you have to do." says Eunice.

Soon, with Chris' help and the help of several friends, Eunice saw the business starting to grow. Outlets for the wine increased and were as far away as Raleigh and Waynesville. Mail order also increased with the help of a web site that Chris created. They found the perfect outlet for a small display and tasting counter at the Hickory Furniture Mart, with lots of people shopping there from all over the country. They changed the name of the company to North Carolina Waldensian Products and 1997 turned out to be a good year. Eunice says Leonard would have been pleased.

Despite the age old myth of mothers-in-law and sons-in-law not getting along, Eunice says she and Chris work well together. He and wife Amy, Eunice's daughter live next door, "but I don't bother them." says Eunice. "I let them have their lives and I have mine, and we get along fine."

As for future growth of the company, Eunice is conservative. The wine is popular and sells quickly. Since they do all the work themselves, they don't want to over extend and find that they can't meet the demand. "We don't want to get any bigger than what we can take care of." she says. From here on, it's a straight forward story.

Directions
Take I-40 exit 125 and go south 1/4 mile to Highway 70. Turn left onto 70 and go east just past Valley Hills Mall to the Furniture Mart on your right.

Wine List

White Wines
Dry Scuppernong - dry fragrant white wine made from Carlos grapes.

Soft Scuppernong - medium sweet white wine made from the Magnolia grape.

Scuppernong - sweet white wine made from 100% Scuppernong grapes.

Blush Wines
Scuppernong Blush - medium sweet blush colored wine made from a special blend of Scuppernong and Muscadine grapes.

Dry Scuppernong Blush - a medium dry blend of Scuppernong and Muscadine grapes.

Red Wines
Dry Muscadine - medium dry, made entirely from the native Muscadine grape.

Sweet Muscadine - sweet red wine made from a traditional southern recipe using only the Muscadine grape.

Sparkling Wines
"Champagne" - semi-sweet and bubbly made from the Scuppernong grape. Naturally fermented in the bottle the "old timey way". (Limited availability. Special orders only.)

Non-Alcoholic Sparkling Ciders
Sparkling Scuppernong Clear Cider - called the "champagne" of gourmet sparkling ciders, this cider is a gentle blend of Scuppernong and Muscadines grapes and apples and is a traditional southern favorite.

Sparkling Scuppernong Blush Cider - similar to the Sparkling Scuppernong Clear Cider but with just a touch of Rougeon grapes for a distinctive color and flavor.

Sparkling Apple Cider - made from a blend of Red Delicious and Winesap apples from the mountains of North Carolina. Only pure juice is used with no sugars or preservatives added.

Sparkling Mulled Apple Cider - cinnamon and cloves are added to the Sparkling Apple Cider to create this delicious cider. Try this warm on chilly evenings.

Eunice discusses the merits of her wines with Ellen Stelling and Gregory Ohlsen of Santa Fe, New Mexico.

While You're Here

Hickory is part of the famous North Carolina furniture country, so be prepared for some power shopping. It also lies on the upper edge of the Piedmont and affords many opportunities for outdoor pursuits.

Hickory

Hickory Metro Convention & Visitors Bureau
(800) 849-5093 (toll free), (828) 322-1335, Fax (828) 328-1175
e-mail: hickory_cvb@w3link.com

Hickory Furniture Mart
2220 Hwy. 70 SE
Hickory, NC 28602
Four floors (17 acres) of furniture, carpets and home decorating ideas.
(800) 462-MART (6278) (toll free), (828) 322-3510
e-mail: inquiries@hfm.pdial.interpath.net
Web site: www.hickoryfurniture.com

Catawba Valley Furniture Museum
Hickory Furniture Mart
Explores the early roots of furniture in the region. Period pieces, early workshop, videos and more. Free
(800) 462-6278 (toll free), (828) 322-3510, Fax (828) 322-6286

Hickory Museum of Art
243 Third Avenue NE
Hickory, NC 28601
Second oldest art museum in North Carolina, and the first in the Southeast to collect American art. Located in the Arts and Science Center of Catawba Valley. Free
(828) 327-8576, Fax (828) 327-7281
e-mail: HMA@w3link.com

Interesting Eats in Hickory

Old Hickory Brewery (Brew Pub)
2828 Highway 70 West
Hickory, NC 28602
(828) 323-8753

Vintage House
271 Third Avenue NW
Hickory, NC 28601
(828) 324-1210

Catawba County

Murray's Mill
1489 Murray's Mill Road
Catawba, NC 28609
Early 20th Century grist mill featuring one of the largest water wheels in the state, plus general store, folk art museum and restored residence of the owner/miller.
(828) 465-0383 Catawba Historical Association

Bunker Hill Covered Bridge
Hwy. 70
Claremont, NC 28610
One of only two remaining covered bridges in North Carolina, the 85 foot span was constructed in 1894. Listed on the National Register of Historic Places. Free
(828) 465-0383

Catawba County Museum of History
30 N. College Avenue
Newton, NC 28658
Housed in the former Catawba County Courthouse, a National Register structure built in 1924, the museum is regional in its scope of the history of Catawba County. Free
(828) 465-0383

Iredell County - Statesville

Fort Dobbs State Historic Site
438 Ft. Dobbs Road
Site of French and Indian War fort. Archaeological sites, displays of artifacts, nature trails and recreational facilities. Free
(704) 873-5866, Fax (704) 873-5866

Bed & Breakfast Inns in Statesville

Cedar Hill Farm Bed & Breakfast
778 Elmwood Road
Statesville, NC 28677
(800) 948-4423 (toll free), (828) 873-4332

"*Good wine and
good fellowship
are the ingredients
of a happy social life.*"
*- Joel Dalmas
Waldensian Heritage Wines*

North Carolina
The Mountains

Joel Dalmas demonstrates a traditional Waldensian crushing tool at the Waldensian Heritage Winery.

Waldensian Heritage Wines

Joel Dalmas, Dr. Joe Jacumin, Carlie Caruso, Dennis Perrou Powell,
Thomas Garrou, Freddy Leger and John Bounous
4940 Villar Lane NE
Valdese, North Carolina 28690
(828) 879-3202

Opening Hours: Friday - Sunday 1:00 to 6:00 p.m.

T o understand the wine making tradition of Valdese, you have to go back to 12th Century Italy. The first records of the Waldensian Church appear in 1183, although it could have formed as early as 400 A. D.. Today it is known to be the oldest evangelical church in existence, but for several hundred years, its members were persecuted as heretics by the Roman Catholic Church. Eventually the Waldensian people fled to the Cottian Alps where they carved out an existence in the high valleys on the border of France. There they became known as the "People of the Valleys," retaining their Italian heritage, but gradually adopting a form of the French language. It wasn't until 1848 that King Charles Albert of Sardinia, in the Edict of Emancipation, granted the Waldensians the same political and legal rights as other citizens. Though not a declaration of religious freedom, the Edict did allow Waldensians to organize congregations and conduct evangelistic and educational activity outside their valleys.

However, with peace and freedom came population growth, and soon the land that had so long been their refuge could no longer support them. The Waldensians began emigrating to places where they could find opportunities to earn a better living.

In 1893 the first of the Waldensian settlers from the Italian Piedmont arrived in the North Carolina Piedmont and founded the village of Valdese. By the end of that year Valdese records showed a total of 222 people, making it the largest Waldensian colony in the world outside of Italy. They brought with them their old world traditions and skills. They were known as excellent rock masons, able to fit together roughly cut stones like jigsaw pieces without the use of mortar. They also made excellent wine.

Today you can see the evidence of the masons' skills in buildings scattered around the village. A few families still make wine for personal use, but it is at Waldensian Heritage Wines that you can experience the wine makers' skills first hand.

Waldensian Heritage Wines is an authentic Waldensian winery producing a variety of Waldensian heritage wines made from grapes similar to those grown in northern Italy. Time consuming old world methods combined with modern innovation preserve the wine making skills of these hardy Italian settlers. The wines have a strong bouquet that displays a true taste of the grape. Altogether, the owners have a combined 250 years of experience in wine making.

As a first generation American, Joel Dalmas spoke no English until he started school in the 1920's. Even then, English was reserved for school or outside situations. "I spoke French to all of the older people, always." explains Joel. "Speaking English would have been considered disrespectful." Valdese was a true colony in those days, preserving its language as well as its old world skills.

"Waldensians have always made wine," says Joel. "We all helped with harvest and crush. Wine making was part of our lives." Joel can show you pictures on the walls of the winery depicting those early days, including one when he was a little child helping with the harvest.

Prior to World War II, the winery at Waldensian Heritage Wines had been the dairy barn for the Dalmas farm. Joel says that when he and others returned from the war, many things had changed in the area, including the number of people making wine. He and four friends decided to get together and form a cooperative for the purpose of making wine and preserving the Waldensian wine making heritage. The five, Joel, Dr. Joe Jacumin, Ernest Jahier, J. P. Dalmas, Joel's brother, and O. H. Pons, Jr., became fondly known as the "Bosses" of the Buonvino ("Good Wine") Family.

They worked together over the years, and were often joined by friends and neighbors for harvests, crush, bottling or whatever needed to be done. "When you start making wine, it's like a magnet for all the friends and neighbors," says Joel. "It's always a party atmosphere." He says it's still the same today. "When we have a Waldensian work party, we take a couple of Waldensian breaks, and we don't serve coffee." In 1989, the Buonvino Family decided to take the venture commercial.

Joel is quick to point out that Waldensian Heritage Wines are true, old world wines. They are made primarily from Niagara and Concord grapes which they buy in the Finger Lakes district of New York state. They used to grow their own grapes years ago but couldn't produce enough to keep up with the demand for their wine. Each year they truck in about 15 tons of grapes, which makes about 2,600 gallons or about 1,100 cases.

When you visit, you'll want to take the tour of the production and storage facilities housed in the old barn along with the winery. You'll get an historical perspective of the community and the wine making operation as well as insight as to just how creative people can be. Joel explains how the wine is made and how expensive some commercial equipment is. As a result, using plastic piping, hoses and hardware store fittings, several machines used in wine production at Waldensian Heritage Wines have either been built to specifications or invented to fill the need.

Private events such as parties, weddings, family reunions and meetings can be scheduled at the winery, but no food is provided. Guests are welcome to bring picnics or have food catered. There are tables and chairs both inside the winery, and outside overlooking a vineyard planted a few years ago to provide atmosphere and grapes for promotional use.

Joel is a wealth of wine information and will tell you how to store wine, pour wine and chill wine, and he explains the sugar content of the wines and how best to drink them. With a sense of humor as dry as his wines Joel will tell you never to drink sweet wine before a meal. "Remember your mother said not to eat sweets before supper." Then, if you want to join the winery "Bosses" and be a part of Waldensian Heritage Wines, Joel will tell you that "you don't go fishing, you don't play golf and you have to have a little bit of Waldensian blood."

Directions
From I-40, take exit 112 and head north until you reach Main Street. Cross Main

Street and continue north about 1.3 miles to Villar Lane. Turn left and follow the signs to the winery.

Wine List

Burgundy Valdese - the original Waldensian wine. It is a dry wine with a lingering aroma of grapes at harvest time. Best served at room temperature and is excellent with red meat and game.

Burgundy Valdese (Black Cap) - the wine Joel Dalmas' father used to make, even drier than regular Burgundy Valdese with zero residual sugar. For those who like a very dry wine.

Villar Rouge Sweet - a red wine that maintains the best qualities of the Burgundy Valdese, but is sweeter. Especially enjoyable as a dessert or after dinner wine. Serve either at room temperature or slightly chilled.

Blanc Royal - the traditional Waldensian white wine, made from a blend of choice white grapes. A semi-dry wine with a well balanced bouquet and a delicate fruity flavor. An excellent choice with appetizers, seafood or poultry. Serve slightly chilled.

Waldensian White Sweet - an artful blend of American and hybrid grapes to produce a soft white wine that can be enjoyed before, during, or after dinner. A truly all-occasion wine. Best served chilled.

Blush Regal - a delightfully pleasant medium dry wine. Produced by limiting the contact between the juice and grape skins, giving the wine its pink color. It is great as a summer sipper, an appetite stimulant and an excellent complement to any meal. Serve slightly chilled.

Piedmont Rose - the newest wine, for people who prefer a sweet wine that maintains its fruitiness and delicate bouquet. Best served chilled.

While You're Here

Burke County is on the eastern edge of the North Carolina mountains and is just minutes away from all the beauty and adventure of the high country. Lots of history and shopping will keep you busy for days.

Burke County
Burke County Travel & Tourism Visitor Center
102 E. Union Street, Courthouse Square
Morganton, NC 28655
(888) 462-2921 (toll free), (828) 433-6793, Fax (828) 433-6715
Internet Address: http://hci.net/~bcttc/

Lake James State Park
Located in western Burke County.
565 acres, campsites and boat landings, picnic areas, canoe rentals
(828) 652-5047

Pisgah National Forest
Linville Gorge Wilderness Area
State Road 1238 off State Road 183
10,975 acres of rugged terrain and scenic beauty.
District Ranger (828) 652-2144

South Mountains State Park
Located in southwestern Burke County off Highway 18
Hiking, camping, horseback riding, mountain biking, picnicking, nature study
(828) 433-4772

Blue Ridge Parkway
North of Morganton; Bisects State Road 181
Designated one of the most scenic by-ways in the United States
(828) 298-0398 Information Line

Catawba River Canoe Trips
CBS.Sports
911 N. Green Street
Morganton, NC 28655
Four hour trip includes escort, life jackets, canoes and transportation
(828) 437-7016

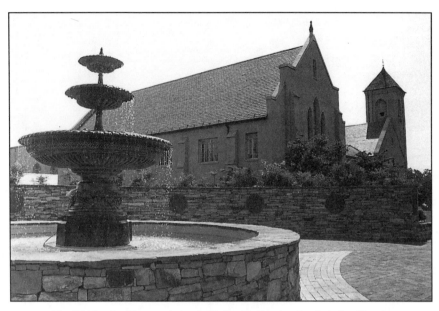
The Waldensian Museum is located in the Waldensian Presbyterian Church.

Valdese
Visitor Information Center
152 E. Main Street/P. O. Box 1256
Valdese, NC 28690
(800) 635-4778 (toll free), (828) 874-1893
e-mail: valdese@ci.valdese.nc.us

Waldensian Museum
101 Rodoret Street SE
Artifacts and exhibits depicting the history of the early Italian settlers.
(828) 874-2531

From This Day Forward
Old Colony Amphitheater on Church Street
Outdoor drama tells the story of the pre-Reformation persecution of the
Waldensians and their struggle to succeed.
(800) 743-8398 (toll free) Old Colony Players

Trail of Faith
Old Colony amphitheater on Church Street
Outdoor exhibit that tells of the persecution and migration of the
Waldensian people.
(828) 874-1893

Meytre's Grist Mill at McGalliard Falls
Church Road
Community park features replica of a grist mill and 45 foot waterfall, nature trails, tennis courts and picnic area.

Old Rock School Auditorium & Art Gallery
Main Street, West
Constructed from stones pulled from the fields, it houses exhibits from local artists and hosts concerts and plays.
(828) 879-2129

Interesting Eats in Valdese

Myra's Ice Cream & Sandwich Shop
212 W. Main Street
Valdese, NC 28690
(828) 879-8049 or (828) 879-8058

Morganton
Old Burke County Courthouse
Courthouse Square
Built in 1837, it houses the Historic Burke Foundation, the Heritage Museum and the Visitor Center.
(828) 437-4104 Historic Burke Foundation

Quaker Meadows Plantation
St. Mary's Church Road
Federal style brick plantation house built in 1812
(828) 437-4104

Quaker Meadows Cemetery
Off Independence Blvd. Near Freedom High School
Earliest identified site associated with white settlement in western North Carolina.
(828) 437-4104

Senator Sam J. Ervin, Jr. Library
Western Piedmont Community College Library
Replica of the late Senator Ervin's home library.

Jailhouse Gallery
115 E. Meeting Street *(cont. on next page)*

Home of the Burke County Arts Council. Renovated jail now hosts art and craft shows of local artists
(828) 433-7282

Brown Mountain Lights
Overlooks located on Highway 181 North
Mysterious lights of unknown origin appear on Brown Mountain. Visible on clear nights.

Apple Hill Orchard & Cider Mill
South of I-40 off Enola Road
Harley Prewitt, owner
5205 Appletree Lane
Morganton, NC 28655
Family owned orchard with 12 varieties of apples, jams and home made ciders. Seasonal
(828) 437-1224

Bed and Breakfast Inns in Burke County

Robardajen Woods B&B
5640 Robardajen Woods
Nebo, NC 28761
(828) 584-3191

Burleson House
200 Lenoir Street
Morganton, NC 28655
(828) 437-5356

BJ's Bed & Breakfast
7348 Joe Johnson Road
Jonas Ridge, NC 28641
(828) 733-0342

Interesting Eats in Morganton

Judges Riverside
128 Greenlee Ford Road
Morganton, NC 28655
(828) 433-5798

Hursey's Bar-B-Que Restaurant
(North Carolina bar-b-que)
300 Carbon City Road (Hwy. 70, West)
Morganton, NC 28655
(828) 437-3001

King Street Cafe
207 S. King Street
Morganton, NC 28655
(828) 437-4477

Perk Place
114 S. Sterling Street
Morganton, NC 28655
(828) 433-8919

Teensy Winery

Bob and Stephanie Howard
Route 1, Box 388-H
Union Mills, North Carolina 28167
(828) 287-7763

Opening Hours: By appointment only

It started in the Chardonnay and slowly spread to the Cabernet and the Merlot. An insidious plague that he fought day and night, but it was no use. A vintner's nightmare; a wine maker's disaster; Black Rot was poised to take over the vineyard and there was no stopping it.

It may sound like a B-grade Hollywood horror movie, but Bob Howard is determined to change the plot of this disaster picture. Armed with a three gallon back pack style spray tank filled with an industry standard fungicide, Bob is prepared to save his 10 year old vineyard, kill the monster and win the day.

"If I had it to do over again, I wouldn't have the Chardonnay at all. This is where the trouble started," Bob explains. We are standing in his vineyard on the side of Chalk Mountain in the Blue Ridge foothills. It's hot. The bugs are biting, and the tiny grapes are showing definite signs of black spots. "I'm working on it a little bit differently this year. I'm attacking it more vigorously and it's taking its toll on me." says Bob. "It's a tremendous amount of work, but I think I'll be able to curtail it."

For two years Bob has been unable to harvest enough grapes to make wine. He's made some jellies, but many of the grapes on his 500 vines have been lost to the fungus. He's determined to turn that around. It takes 8 trips up and down the mountain for one 30 gallon spraying. Then he has to do it all over again. The vines themselves are full and healthy, so he knows he can lick the problem. It's just a matter of time.

The Teensy Winery is the smallest bonded winery in North Carolina and normally produces about 150 cases of Chardonnay and Cabernet Sauvignon per year. Locals will tell you it's some of the best wine around.

An insurance agent by profession, a wine maker by hobby, Bob had always wanted to start a vineyard. When the local college asked him to teach a course on wine making, he jumped at the chance. He taught the course and had a lot fun with it. In the meantime he ordered the paperwork to get his vineyard started. Then he thought about it for a year. When he finally decided to give it a try, the forms had been changed, so he had to order a whole new set of forms.

"We went back and forth for months before everything was signed, sealed and stamped." says Bob. "This is a business that takes a long time. I started this when I was in my early 40's. I've been in it for over ten years. Your vines take three years. In the fourth year, you can produce. Then it's another five years to get it on the market. You have to ask yourself, do you really want to do this?"

If the answer is yes, Bob says the first thing to do is learn how to grow grapes. Learn as much as you can about vines. Get a subscription to the local agriculture department newsletter and build your library. Reading is fundamental. Look for used equipment from businesses that are closing such as stainless steel tanks from dairies. It's a lot of work.

So why make wine? Self gratification and having fun says Bob.

"You get to get outside. You get some hard work involved in what you do. It's a diversion from the everyday paper pushing." he says. It's also a great way for a runner to get out of the office. When he isn't running up and down the mountain spraying vines, Bob runs races such as the 10,000 meter Cooper River Run in Charleston, South Carolina. He also runs races in Charlotte, Maggie Valley and Rutherfordton. But his biggest race at the moment is against time and nature, in the vineyard.

"I think this year I'll get rid of the Black Rot. It's slowing down. I've pretty well stymied it." says Bob. Things are looking good. If so, there will once again be a Teensy bit of wine.

Directions

From Interstate 40, take the Rutherfordton exit. Go south on U.S. Highway 221 to Thermal City. Turn right on to State Road 1321 and head west to State Road 1328, also called Painter's Gap Road. Turn right on to Painter's Gap Road. The Teensy Winery is the first road on the left after you pass Welcome Home Baptist Church.

From Rutherfordton, go north on U. S. Highway 221 to Gilkey. Turn left on to State Road 1328 and follow it about 5 miles. The Teensy Winery is the first road on the left after you pass Welcome Home Baptist Church.

Wine List

Chardonnay - crisp and dry with a hint of citrus

Cabernet Sauvignon - rich and full bodied, a robust red

A rock wall that Bob built by hand separates the backyard of his home from the vineyard.

While You're Here

This is a scenic part of the state and accessible to many activities from water sports to museum hopping. Don't miss the shops of Chimney Rock Village for quaint, North Carolina mountain made gifts. Definitely vacation country.

Rutherford County Tourism Development Authority
162 N. Main Street
Rutherfordton, NC 28139
(800) 849-5998 (toll free), (828)286-1110
Web site: www.blueridge.net/tda

Rutherfordton
Green River Plantation
Cox Road
Historic plantation circa 1804. Call for directions, prices, times and reservations.
(828) 286-1461 or (828) 287-0983

Thermal City Gold Mine
5240 U. S. Highway 221, N
Union Mills, NC 28167
Relive the gold rush days with recreational mining and on site prospecting at an active gold mine. RV park, primitive camping, gem mine, rock shop, on the Second Broad River.
(828) 286-3016

Bed & Breakfast Inns in Rutherfordton

Pinebrae Manor
Hwy. 108 (RR#5), Box 479-A
Rutherfordton, NC 28139
(828) 286-1543

Carrier House Bed & Breakfast
249 & 255 N. Main Street
Rutherfordton, NC 28139
(828) 287-4222

Interesting Eats in Rutherfordton

On the Boardwalk
Oak Springs Road
Rutherfordton, NC 28139
(828) 287-2932

Lake Lure

Hickory Nut Gorge Visitor Center
U. S. Highways 64/74
Lake Lure, NC 28746
Information on Gerton, Chimney Rock, Bat Cave, and Lake Lure. Boating, swimming, beautiful scenery. Much of the movie "Dirty Dancing" was filmed here.
(828) 625-2725

Lake Lure Tours
P. O. Box 541
Scenic cruises on beautiful Lake Lure. Also specialty cruises, dinner cruises and private charters.
(828) 625-0077, Fax (828) 625-8081
e-mail: skipper@lakelure.com
Web site: www.lakelure.com

Bottomless Pools
U. S. Highways 64/74
Twenty minute walking tour includes three waterfalls and pools.
(828) 625-8324

*A breathtaking view of Lake Lure and the surrounding
area awaits you at Chimney Rock Park.*

Cedar Creek Stables & Outfitters, Inc.
530 Cedar Creek Road (off Bills Creek Road)
Lake Lure, NC 28746
Mountain trail rides, riding lessons, fishing lake, gem mine and pony rides.
Genuine working farm.
(828) 625-2811

Bed & Breakfast Inns in Lake Lure

Gäestehaus Salzburg Bed & Breakfast
1491 Memorial Highway
Lake Lure, NC 28746
(828) 625-0093, Fax (828) 625-0091

Lodge on Lake Lure
Charlotte Drive, off Highways 64/74
P. O. Box 519
Lake Lure, NC 28746
(800) 733-2785 (toll free), (828) 625-2789, Fax (828) 625-2421

Interesting Eats in Lake Lure

Mimi's Tea Room
U. S. Highways 64/74 A (behind Lake Lure Inn)
Lake Lure, NC 28746
(828) 625-TEAS (8327)

Chimney Rock
Chimney Rock Park
U. S. Highways 64/74/P. O. Box 39
Chimney Rock, NC 28720
A 26 story elevator ride through a tunnel surrounded by solid granite takes you to Chimney Rock level, with its breathtaking 75 mile view of the Blue Ridge. Three nature trails lead you to a 404 foot waterfall.
(800) 277-9611 (toll free)
Web site: www.visit@chimneyrockpark.com

Bed & Breakfast Inns in Chimney Rock

Wicklow Inn
U. S. Hwy. 64/74 A
Chimney Rock, NC 28720 *(cont. on next page)*

(877) 625-4038 (toll free), (828) 625-4038
Web site: www.chimney-rock.com/wicklow-inn.htm

The Dogwood Inn Bed & Breakfast
U. S. Highways 64/74 A/P. O. Box 159
Chimney Rock, NC 28720
(800) 992-5557 (toll free), (828) 625-4403, Fax (828) 625-8825
e-mail: dogwoodinn@blueridge.net
Web site: www.blueridge.net/~dogwoodinn

Interesting Eats in Chimney Rock

Genny's Family Restaurant
& Gift Shop
451 Main Street
Chimney Rock, NC 28720
(828) 625-2171

Rocky River Ice Cream
& Fudge
430 Main Street
Chimney Rock, NC 28720
(828) 625-9534

Rutherfordton County
Shakespeare's Globe Theatre in America Project
P. O. Box 44,
Forest City, NC 28043
On going educational and theatrical project to bring Shakespeare's Globe Theatre to North Carolina. Reconstruction of Elizabethan wooden buildings that housed Shakespeare's theatre, Shakespeare's plays performed on an outdoor stage. Visitors' Center includes historical exhibits. Located across from Town Hall in Alexander Mills, North Carolina.
(828) 248-1000

Rutherford County Museum
102 West Main Street
Forest City, NC 28043
Permanent art exhibits, mineral, fossil and sea life exhibits, Native American artifacts and crafts.
(828) 245-4000

Library of Old Tryon Genealogical Society
102 West Main Street
Forest City, NC 28043
Genealogy library open to the public. Open Wednesday and Thursday 9:00 a.m. to 2:00 p.m.
(828) 248-4010

"Here with a Loaf of Bread
beneath the bough,
A Flask of Wine, a Book of
Verse - and Thou
Beside me singing in the
Wilderness -
And Wilderness is Paradise enow."
- Edward Fitzgerald
The Rubaiyat of Omar Khayyam

Biltmore Estate Winery
(Located on Biltmore Estate)

Mailing Address:
One North Pack Square
Asheville, North Carolina 28801
(800) 543-2961 (toll free)

Winery Opening Hours:
January - March, Monday - Saturday 11:00 a.m. to 6:00 p.m.
Sunday 12:00 noon - 6:00 p.m.
April - December, Monday - Saturday 11:00 a.m. to 7:00 p.m.
Sunday 12:00 noon - 7:00 p.m.

Estate Entrance and Ticket Center Hours:*
January - March, Daily 9:00 a.m. to 5:00 p.m.
April - December, Daily 8:30 a.m. to 5:00 p.m.

Biltmore House Hours: Year Round Daily 9:00 a.m. to 6:00 p.m.
Closed Thanksgiving Day and Christmas Day

*Note - One entry fee is charged that covers the House, Gardens and Winery. It seems a bit high, but there's lots to do. Biltmore Estate is self supporting and receives no government funding. Therefore, admissions play a vital role in the preservation of the house and grounds.

Like most 20-Somethings, George wanted a place of his own; a place where he could have friends over for parties; a place where he could have his own stuff and create his own style; a place where he didn't have to depend on anyone else, where he could be his own boss. He knew it would be the most fabulous place anyone had ever seen.

Unlike most 20-Somethings, George had the money, the manpower, the education and the sophistication to do it. He found just the right spot and started buying the land, lots of land, for this 20-Something was the grandson of "Commodore" Cornelius Vanderbilt, patriarch of the fabulous Vanderbilt family of New York.

Born in 1862, George Washington Vanderbilt III was the youngest of William Henry and Maria Louisa Vanderbilt's eight children. He was a quiet, intellectual child whose interests included art, literature and horticulture. He first traveled to Europe at age 10 and fell in love with the architecture of the French châteaux. Influenced by his father, he began collecting books and art at an early age, dreaming of the day he would create a fabulous place to house them.

That day came in 1888 when he visited Asheville, North Carolina, a popular health resort at the time. He knew immediately that it was here he wanted to build his home and purchased a total of 125,000 acres. He called the estate "Biltmore" from "Bildt," the Dutch town from which his ancestors had come, and "more," an old English word for open, rolling land.

Much of the land had been clear cut, a common 19th century practice when trees were so abundant as to appear to be in endless supply. This meant he could create farms, parkland, and new forests, just the sort of projects to keep a horticulturist occupied. He hired landscape architect Frederick Law Olmsted, today known as the founding father of American landscape architecture and the designer of New York's Central Park, to create a place of beauty as well as a useful, self-sustaining European-style estate. George practiced sustainable living 100 years ahead of his time.

Meanwhile, for the house and other structures he hired renowned architect Richard Morris Hunt. Construction of the house began in 1889 and took 1000 artisans six years to complete. George and Richard traveled Europe and Asia on shopping sprees, purchasing carpets, furniture, antique tapestries, china, and art for the French Renaissance-style château. When it was completed, the house was more than a mansion. It was a fabulous palace with 250 rooms including 35 bedrooms, 43 bathrooms, 65 fireplaces, three kitchens, and an indoor swimming pool and a bowling alley. It boasted all the latest modern conveniences including Thomas Edison's electric light bulbs, hot and cold running water, central heat, a fire alarm system, two elevators and an electric call box system for the servants. It even had a telephone. Biltmore was one of the most technologically advanced structures of its time.

George was very committed to the idea of a self-sustaining estate and spent much of his time planning new ways to make it happen. Vegetables and fruit were grown on the Estate and cattle and sheep were raised there. Biltmore made its own bread and had its own dairy that sold milk, cheese, butter and delicious ice cream.

It wasn't until 76 years later that George's grandson, William Amherst Vanderbilt Cecil, planted grape vines on the Estate. At first he experimented with native grapes, but decided that vinifera grapes were more in keeping with the Biltmore concept of the French country estate. He brought in French master winemaker Philippe Jourdain and Biltmore sold its first vintage in 1979.

That same year, the dairy became a separate business managed by William's brother, George Cecil. Plans were made to renovate the dairy barn and turn it into a winery. Today, the 96,500 square foot structure, one of the original estate buildings designed by Richard Morris Hunt, houses Biltmore's state-of-the-art wine production, Tasting Room and Wine Shop.

Opened to the public in 1985, Biltmore's Winery is the most visited winery in America, hosting 500,000 guests each year. More than 75,000 cases of fine wines are produced annually and sold in six Southeastern states. 51,500 vines grow on 72 acres on the west banks of the French Broad River, making Biltmore's vineyards one of the largest vinifera plantings east of the Mississippi. In addition, grapes that don't grow well in the region, such as Zinfandel, Chenin Blanc and Sauvignon Blanc, are purchased from vineyards in California and Washington to complete Biltmore's selection of varietals and blends. Over the years, Biltmore wines have garnered over 150 awards at national and international competitions, including two Double Gold medals.

Guests can tour the winery at their own pace. The Winery Welcome Center has ever changing displays and serves as a starting point. You can view crush at harvest time and learn how the wine goes from the vine to the bottle. A 7-minute video tells the Biltmore wine story and interactive displays on Scholars' Walk give you more details on grape growing. You'll see the fermentation rooms where the wine is stored in stainless steel tanks or oak barrels depending on the type of wines, and the champagne bottling room. Go underground and roam the tunnels, originally used for cleaning the dairy and transporting milk. Today they are perfect wine cellars. Back in the daylight you can sip Biltmore wines at your leisure in the Tasting Room and browse the extensive Wine Shop. Two huge rooms offer wines and non-alcoholic sparkling ciders, glassware, books, baskets, Estate jams and jellies, accessories, and a variety of foods. You can put together a whole picnic to take on to the Estate grounds, or into the Winery Courtyard if you prefer.

There's always something going on at Biltmore's Winery. Throughout the year, live music, grape stomping, children's crafts, and wine tastings coordinate with Estate events such as *Festival of Flowers* and *Christmas at Biltmore Estate* celebrations. During the summer months, the Winery presents event weekends on Memorial Day, July 4th and Labor Day. Private wine tastings can be scheduled by contacting Biltmore Estate's Group Sales office

Today, Biltmore Estate comprises 8,000 acres of formal gardens, wooded hillsides and farmland. Much of the original land was sold to the federal government in the early 20th Century by

Grape harvest at
Biltmore Estate.

George's widow, Edith, as a tribute to his commitment to preservation. That land is the nucleus of the Pisgah National Forest. If you go south of Asheville on the Blue Ridge Parkway, you'll come to Buck Spring Overlook, elevation 4,980 feet, where George kept a hunting lodge. Come back to Asheville on the Parkway and on your last descent you'll spot Biltmore House, rising out of the surrounding forest. Covering four acres of floor space, the house remains the largest private residence in the country. Binoculars or a strong telephoto lens on your camera afford a great view.

George Washington Vanderbilt III's dream of a working estate became a reality in 1895. Over 100 years later the one constant has remained; that the Estate is a self-supporting agricultural endeavor. Fruit and vegetables, cattle and wine are all products of the land and they echo Frederick Law Olmsted's words, "To be beautiful, land must be useful."

Directions
From I-40, take exit 50 or 50-B at U.S. Highway 25. Follow the Biltmore Estate signs to the entrance (about 1 mile north of the Interstate).

Wine List

White Wines - Serve chilled

Sauvignon Blanc Special Reserve - this, the driest selection on the wine list, has delightful aromas of citrus and grapefruit with hints of creamy oak and a refreshing, elegant acidity. Enjoy with lighter dishes or on its own.

Sauvignon Blanc - a classic dry wine, full bodied with a pleasant finish. Aged for a few months in small oak barrels, this wine is yellow straw in color and exhibits a floral and exotic fruit aroma with hints of vanilla. Goes especially well with seafood.

Chardonnay Sur Lies - this dry Chardonnay was created by allowing the young wine to age on its sediment during the fall and winter. This "Sur Lies" process adds a subtle fruit aroma and a pleasant, complex character. The wine complements a wide variety of foods and is ideal with salads and light dishes such as veal, poultry, ham and seafood.

Chardonnay # 21 - this semi-sweet wine is ideal with poultry, especially sweet and sour dishes, and pasta.

Johannisberg Riesling - this wine possesses a very floral and spicy aroma, combined with a crisp, spicy taste. Serve as an aperitif, with cold vegetable soups or fruit tarts and pastries.

Chenin Blanc - a full bodied, flavorful varietal accentuated by a sweet finish. Great for sipping or served with desserts.

Special Reserve Chenin Blanc - made from very ripe grapes, this is a sweet wine with a rich golden color and a tropical bouquet. The wonderful balance and lingering finish makes this an ideal dessert wine.

Selected wines from each vintage are stored for the future.

Rosé Wines - Serve chilled
Zinfandel Blanc De Noir - a complex wine with aromas hinting of cherry, lemon and raspberry and offering the balance of a pleasant sweetness with a strength of flavor. Its lively character is excellent with spicy and grilled foods and is the perfect addition to summer cookouts and picnics.

Cabernet Blanc De Noir - a light wine made from a dark grape which gives it a brilliant terra-cotta color. Made with North Carolina grapes, its rosy, spicy aromas are rich and well balanced with the semi-sweet fruit flavors. It goes well with quiche, sausages, and sandwiches with white meat. Also, try this wine with any chocolate dessert.

Red Wines - Best when served at temperatures between 59 and 68 degrees Fahrenheit
Cabernet Sauvignon - a rich and elegant wine with the deep red color of dark cherries. It has a complex aroma (bell pepper and black currant) and a flavor that hints of spices and smooth tannins. Complements a variety of meats.

Cardinal's Crest - a master blending of four grapes, including Pinot Noir, this wine is named after the ceremonial wall hangings of the French statesmen, Cardinal Duc de Richelieu (1585-1642), in the Biltmore House Collection. A dry, full-bodied, velvety and smooth wine, it best complements lamb, white meats and fish.

Merlot - this wine presents a soft texture with elegant undertones of spices and plum. Though the rich fruit and structure will age graciously, this wine is ready to enjoy now. Its inherent complexity complements poultry and red meats.

Cerise - Biltmore's newest, medium-bodied red blends six grapes and is aptly named for its cherry color. Smoky aromas of cherry, raspberry and leather lead to a distinctive peppery finish. An excellent complement to Italian pasta or spicy foods.

Other Biltmore wines include the Chateau Biltmore Collection and the collection of sparkling wines produced in the *Methode Champenoise*.

While You're Here

Altitude affects attitude is Asheville's motto, so if your attitude is focused on fun, you'll find it here. Mountains, museums, scenery, shopping, Asheville has it all. Don't miss the downtown historic district with its architectural treasures. Rediscover Asheville's literary legacy through the writings of Thomas Wolfe, O. Henry, and F. Scott Fitzgerald during the annual Thomas Wolfe Festival in October. You might even get to see a movie being filmed as more and more Hollywood producers have discovered the area provides better scenery than a sound stage backdrop. You can visit six North Carolina wineries using Asheville as a base, so plan a vacation, then plan to return.

Asheville

Asheville Convention & Visitors Bureau
P. O. Box 1010
Asheville, NC 28802-1010
(800) 257-1300 (toll free), (828) 258-6101
Web site: www.ashevillechamber.org

Biltmore Village
Adjacent to Biltmore Estate's entrance. Restored 1890's community of fine shops, restaurants and galleries.

Botanical Gardens
151 Weaver Blvd.
Asheville, NC 28804
Ten acres are of native plants just off Broadway on Weaver Boulevard.
(828) 252-5190

Asheville Downtown Association & Historic District
Outstanding collection of early 20th Century architecture including structures on the National Register of Historic Places. 100 retail shops and 40 diverse restaurants.
Guided Walking Tour (828) 259-5855
Special Events (828) 251-9973, Festivals (828) 259-5800

Folk Art Center
Home of the Southern Highland Craft Guild. Features the work of 700 members. At milepost 382 of the Blue Ridge Parkway, just north of U. S. Highway 70 entrance in east Asheville.
(828) 298-7928

Riverside Cemetery
53 Birch Street
Burial place of Thomas Wolfe and O. Henry
(828) 258-8480

Thomas Wolfe Memorial
52 North Market Street
Novelist's boyhood home and setting for "Look Homeward Angel".
(828) 253-8304

Bed & Breakfast Inns in Asheville

Abbington Green Bed & Breakfast
46 Cumberland Circle
Asheville, NC 28801
National Register of Historic Places
(800) 251-2454 (toll free), (828) 251-2454, Fax (828) 251-2872
Web site: www.abbingtongreen.com

Cedar Crest Victorian Inn
674 Biltmore Avenue
Asheville, NC 28803
National Register of Historic Places
(800) 252-0310 (toll free), (828) 252-1389
Web site: www.cedarcrestvictorianinn.com

Chestnut Street Inn
176 E. Chestnut Street
Asheville, NC 28801
(800) 894-2955 (toll free), (828) 285-0705
Web site: www.chestnutstreetinn.com

Hill House Victorian B&B
120 Hillside Street
Asheville, NC 28801
(800) 379-0002 (toll free), (828) 232-0345
Web site: www.bbonline.com/nc/hillhouse

The Lion & The Rose
276 Montford Avenue
Asheville, NC 28801
(800) 546-6988 (toll free), (828) 255-7673
Web site: www.a-o.com/lion-rose

Old Reynolds Mansion
100 Reynolds Heights
Asheville, NC 28804
National Register of Historic Places
(800) 709-0496 (toll free), (828) 254-0496

Interesting Eats in Asheville

Biltmore Dairy Bar
115 Hendersonville Road
Asheville, NC 28803
(828) 274-2370

The Blue Rooster
48 Biltmore Avenue
Asheville, NC 28801
(828) 281-4500

Cafe on the Square
One Biltmore Avenue
Asheville, NC 28801
(828) 251-5565

Wine Shops in Asheville

Asheville Wine Market
65 Biltmore Avenue
Asheville, NC 28801
(828) 253-0060

Black Mountain

Black Mountain/Swannanoa Valley Chamber of Commerce
201 East State Street
Black Mountain, NC 28711
Located 15 miles east of Asheville. Antique and handmade crafts, furniture, factory outlet stores, and restaurants. Take exit 64 off I-40.
(800) 669-2301 (toll free), (828) 669-2300, Fax (828) 669-1407
e-mail: bmchamber@juno.com
Web site: www.blackmountain.org

Bed & Breakfast Inns in Black Mountain

Black Mountain Inn
718 W. Old Hwy. 70
Black Mountain, NC 28711
(800) 735-6128 (toll free), (828) 669-6528

Interesting Eats in Black Mountain

Berliner Kindle German Restaurant & Deli
20 Ball Street
Black Mountain, NC 28711
(828) 669-5255

Green Light Cafe
205 W. State Street
Black Mountain, NC 28711
(828) 669-2444

Black Mountain Bakery
102 Church Street
Black Mountain, NC 28711
(828) 669-1626

Veranda Cafe & Gifts
119 Cherry Street
Black Mountain, NC 28711
(828) 669-8864

Blue Ridge Parkway
Scenic mountain parkway winds 469 miles along the highest ridges from Shenandoah National Park (Virginia) to the Great Smoky Mountains National Park. Parkway intersects Asheville at U.S. Highways 25, 70 and 74, and NC State Road 191.
(828) 298-0398 Information Line

Mount Mitchell State Park
Highest peak east of the Mississippi River. State Park has nature trails, nine primitive tent sites, outlook tower, restaurant, picnic area and museum. Blue Ridge Parkway milepost 355 north east of Asheville.
(828) 675-4611

Weaverville

Vance Birthplace State Historic Site
911 Reems Creek Road
Weaverville, NC 28787
Experience life as an early pioneer at this restored late 18th Century farmstead of North Carolina Senator and Civil War Governor, Zebulon B. Vance. Located on Reems Creek Road off U. S. Highway 25 North
(828) 645-6706

Bed & Breakfast Inns in Weaverville

Dry Ridge Inn
26 Brown Street
Weaverville, NC 28787
(800) 839-3899 (toll free), (828) 658-3899
Web site: www.bbonline.com/nc/dryridge

Interesting Eats in Weaverville

Weaverville Milling Company Restaurant
P. O. Box 26
Weaverville, NC 28787
(828) 645-4700

Guests at Biltmore Estate Winery enjoy sampling wines in the Tasting Room.

*"A meal without wine is like
a day without sunshine."*
- Louis Pasteur

Silohouse Vineyards

Jim and Jennifer Sink
Route 1, Box 408, Walker Road
Waynesville, North Carolina 28786
(828) 452-9666

Opening Hours: By appointment

Jim and Jennifer Sink were living in Tampa, Florida, the "big city," and they were burned out. The traffic, the congestion, the noise, the "rat race" in general had them thinking that there had to be a better way to live. "I'd pick up the newspaper and it seemed that everything I read was negative. I said to my wife, 'Why are we living like this?'"

Jim had always been interested in the procedures involved in producing grapes and creating wine from them, so, he took a trip to Napa Valley, California, to observe the techniques they employ there. After two weeks of visiting the various vineyards and observing the lifestyle of the vintners, a passion began to form. He liked what he saw, and explains. "I had always been interested in growing things, I had just never done it."

He was also interested in wine. "I started my wine drinking career when I was a student at Santa Fe Junior College in Gainesville, Florida," he relates. "To supplement my income I worked in an ABC Liquor store. My manager noticed that there was a new trend in wine drinking, so he set up tastings for the employees to teach us about various wines. We sampled many different varieties, I really favored the darker reds. From that moment on, I began drinking wine whenever we had dinner with friends."

The Sinks owned a summer cottage in the mountains, a former barn complete with a grain silo, that had belonged to Jennifer's grandfather. After the Napa Valley trip, Jim proposed they move to the cottage and give the life of a vintner a try. Jennifer agreed, and in January of 1991, they moved to Waynesville to begin their new life..

"I'm the type of guy that if I make up my mind to do something, I say 'Let's Do it,' and I jump in with both feet." remarks Jim.

He continued his research by contacting the only person in the area that he knew of who was knowledgeable about vinifera grapes and wine making; Master Winemaker Bernard Delille of Biltmore Estate Winery in Asheville, North Carolina. Jim discussed his vision with Bernard who told him, "When you grow your own grapes, come back and see me. I'll teach how to make wine."

"He was testing me to confirm that my wine making intentions were not just fleeting thoughts," Jim explains. "He wanted to see me do something first, to know that I was really serious."

At Bernard's request, Jim met with Martie York, Biltmore Estate Vineyard Manager. "She was a wealth of information. She told me to plant a few vines in a few different varieties to see which ones would grow best in my soil. She said plant 10 or 12 vines - so I planted 1600. I put both feet right in!" Jim exclaims.

The soil on the slope of the mountain where the Sinks live is very rocky. Jim had someone plow the rows for him, then ran a cultivator through them. He began to dig the holes with a post-hole digger. That lasted about two holes. "You can't manually dig through this rock," he says. "It was just me doing all this, so I rented a one-man auger and I wrestled with that for while. That didn't work. As a last resort, I rented a *Bob Cat* with an auger. I said to myself, 'This is what I need - more power!' I started grinding them out and got all 1600 holes dug."

The vines grew, and in 1992 Jim ordered juice from California to begin practicing wine making techniques. He recalls, "Bernard would send me home and I'd do tests on my samples. I'd go back to him and we'd do the tests together to see how I was progressing." Jim's skills improved, and in 1995 he produced 360 gallons of Cabernet and 70 gallons of Chardonnay from his first harvest.

"I found that Cabernet Sauvignon and Chardonnay are the strongest varieties that will grow in this altitude (about 3200 feet) and with the weather conditions we have here. We have an excess of rain, so we're on a heavy disease prevention spray program. The lighter skinned grapes have a tendency to burst and disease gets into them quickly. I also found that for some reason, the Chardonnay doesn't produce as big a cluster or as many grapes in comparison to the Cabernet, regardless of how many spurs I leave on the vines."

The Chardonnay generally comes out in early to mid-April, leaving itself open to frost danger. In both 1996 and 1997 Jim lost his Chardonnay crop to a heavy frost. The Cabernet usually comes out around the beginning of May, after the danger of frost, and produces a lot more fruit.

"I talk to my vines," Jim laughs, "and I tell the Chardonnay it better stay healthy because if it dies, I'm not replanting it. I'll plant Cabernet instead."

Jim continues to work closely with Bernard. Every year he takes a 200 berry sample to Asheville in order to plan the harvest. "He is my mentor," says Jim, "and he's a good friend."

Harvest time is a family and friends affair, and that too is part of the lifestyle Jim and Jennifer want. Their children, Perry and Sara, have settled into the community schools and activities. Jim has plans to plant more vines and increase production over the next few years.

As for the Tampa "rat race," it has become a distant memory, limited to an annual vacation to visit family and friends. Jim goes there on fishing trips and for lobstering in the Keys when the vines require the least amount of tending. Mostly, however, he is content to sip his wine on the deck of his mountain hideaway, overlooking the very thing that made his dream a reality; the vineyard.

"We are having fun here, and I'm happy with the wine that the vines are producing." says Jim. Commenting on the age old debate of which type of wine is best, he offers this insight. "I don't think it's a matter of who is right and who is wrong. It's to the individual's taste; a matter of what pleases your palate. I drink a lot of different wines. I've drunk cheap wines and very expensive wines. There are some wines I really like, but if I'm not drinking those, I might as well be drinking my own - and I do. I'm not saying mine's better than anyone else's, but I like it."

Directions
From Waynesville, take U.S. Highways 23/74 south about four miles. When you come to the large blue Rest Area/Visitor Information sign, there will be a Phillips 66 gas station across the highway on the left. Turn right on Walker Road and go about one mile, past the golf course and past the vineyard to the red mailbox on the right.

Wine List

Cabernet Sauvignon - a bold, full bodied red

Jim Sink
enjoys the view of
his vineyard
and the mountains
at Silohouse
Vineyards.

While You're Here

Haywood County is in the heart of the North Carolina mountains and on the eastern edge of the Great Smoky Mountains National Park, so there's lots to see and do here. Visit famous Maggie Valley, Franklin, Highlands, it's all within reach. Spend an afternoon on a mountain top breathing in the sweet air and savoring the peace and serenity. It will renew your spirit.

Haywood County
Haywood County Tourism Development Authority
"Gateway to the Smokies"
1233 N. Main Street, Suite I-40
Waynesville, NC 28786
(800) 334-9036 (toll free), (828) 452-0152, Fax (828) 452-0153
e-mail: hctda@smokeymountains.net
Web site: www.smokeymountains.net

Maggie Valley Area Chamber of Commerce and Convention and Visitors Bureau
2487 Soco Road
Maggie Valley, NC 28751
(800) 785-8259 (toll free), (828) 926-1686, Fax (828) 926-9396
Web site: www.smokeymountains.net

Cherokee Indian Reservation
Visitors Center
P. O. Box 460
Cherokee, NC 28719
Located at the entrance to both the Great Smoky Mountains National Park and the Blue Ridge Parkway. Cherokee history, culture and art is presented at several museums and attractions on this 56,000 acre reservation
(800) 438-1601 (toll free)
(828) 497-9195
Fax (828) 497-3220
e-mail: chero@drake.dnet.net
Web site: www.cherokee-nc.com

Blue Ridge Parkway
Scenic mountain parkway winds 469 miles along the highest ridges from Shenandoah National Park (Virginia) to the Great Smoky Mountains National Park. Parkway intersects U. S. Highways 23/74 west of Silohouse just past the rest area.
(828) 298-0398 Information Line

Waterfalls are a frequent sight
on the Blue Ridge Parkway.

Great Smoky Mountains National Park
Extends about 70 miles along the North Carolina-Tennessee boarder and contains over one-half million acres of protected forest.
(423) 436-1200

Bed & Breakfast Inns in Clyde

WindDancers Lodging and L'ama Treks
1966 Martins Creek Road
Clyde, NC 28721
(828) 627-6986, Fax (828) 627-0754
e-mail: sgord@primeline.com
Web site: www.winddancersnc.com

Windsong: A Mountain Inn
459 Rockcliffe Lane
Clyde, NC 28721
(828) 627-6111, Fax (828) 627-8080
e-mail: themancinis@compuserve.com
Web site: www.bbonline.com/nc/windsong

Waynesville

Museum of North Carolina Handicrafts
49 Shelton Street
Waynesville, NC 28786
Comprehensive exhibit of heritage crafts includes wood carvings, quilts, pottery, china painting, handcrafted jewelry, Cherokee and Navaho artifacts and some period furniture.
(828) 452-1551

Haywood County Arts Council
37 Church Street
Waynesville, NC 28786
Various exhibits throughout the year. Call for information.
(828) 452-0593

Bed & Breakfast Inns in Waynesville

The Evergreens Bed & Breakfast
724 Smathers Street
Waynesville, NC 28786
(828) 452-0848
e-mail: evergreens@the-evergreens.com
Web site: www.the-evergreens.com

Haywood House Bed & Breakfast
675 S. Haywood Street
Waynesville, NC 28786
(828) 456-9831, Fax (828) 456-4400

Oak Park Inn
314 S. Main Street
Waynesville, NC 28786
(828) 456-5328,
Fax (828) 456-8126

Herren House Bed & Breakfast
94 East Street
Waynesville, NC 28786
(800) 284-1932 (toll free)
Web site: www.circle.net/~herren

Ten Oaks Bed & Breakfast Home
224 Love Lane
Waynesville, NC 28786
National Register of Historic Places
(800) 563-2925 (toll free), (828) 452-9433
e-mail: tenoaks@cheta.net
Web site: www.bbonline.com/nc/tenoaks

Interesting Eats in Waynesville

Angelo's Family Pizza & Italian Restaurant
550 N. Wall Street
Waynesville, NC 28786
(828) 452-1886

Bogart's Restaurant & Tavern
303 S. Main Street
Waynesville, NC 28786
(828) 452-1313

Full Circle Cafe
136 N. Main Street
Waynesville, NC 28786
(828) 456-3050

O'Malley's on Main Pub & Grill
172 N. Main Street
Waynesville, NC 28786
(828) 452-4228

Lomo Grill
121 Church Street
Waynesville, NC 28786
(828) 452-5222

Whitman's Bakery & Sandwich Shoppe
18 N. Main Street
Waynesville, NC 28786
(828) 456-8271

Jackson County
Jackson County Chamber of Commerce
116 Central Street
Sylva, NC 28779
(800) 962-1911 (toll free), (828) 586-2155, Fax (828) 586-4887
e-mail: jctta@nc-mountains.com
Web site: www.nc-mountains.com

Unto These Hills Outdoor Drama
U. S. Highway 441 at Drama Road/P. O. Box 398
Cherokee, NC 28719
For nearly 50 years this outdoor drama has portrayed the history of the

Cherokee Nation covering the period of 1540 up to and through their removal to Indian territory in Oklahoma.
(828) 497-2111, Fax (828) 497-6987

Dillsboro
Great Smoky Mountains Railway
119 Front Street/P. O. Box 397
Dillsboro, NC 28725-0397
Real train travels through river gorges, tunnels and valleys. Dinner and holiday excursions.
(800) 872-4681 (toll free), (828) 586-8811, Fax (828) 586-8806
Web site: www.gsmr.com

Bed & Breakfast Inns in Dillsboro

Applegate Inn Bed & Breakfast
163 Hemlock Street/P. O. Box 1051
Dillsboro, NC 28725
(828) 586-2397, Fax (828) 631-9010
e-mail: applegate@wcu.campus.mci.net
Web site: www.virtualcities.com

Horseback riding in the Great Smoky Mountains National Park.

Olde Towne Inn Bed & Breakfast
300 Haywood Road
Dillsboro, NC 28725
(828) 586-3461
e-mail: Lera_Chitwood@prodigy.net
Web site: www.bbonline.com/nc/oldetown

The Jarrett House
100 Haywood Street
Dillsboro, NC 28725
(800) 972-5623 (toll free), (828) 586-0265, Fax (828) 586-6251
Web site: preation.com/jarretthouse/

Interesting Eats in Dillsboro

Dillsboro Steak & Seafood House
489 Haywood Road
Dillsboro, NC 28725
(828) 586-8934

Sylva
Chief Saunookes Bear Park
Oconee Road
Features a variety of bears. Includes a small petting zoo.
(828) 497-5836

Bed & Breakfast Inns in Sylva

Sans Souci Bed & Breakfast
1068 Monteith Branch Road
Sylva, NC 28779
(828) 586-2645

Bed & Breakfast Inns in Balsam

Balsam Mountain Inn
Seven Springs Road
Balsam, NC 28707
(800) 224-9498 (toll free), (828) 456-9498, Fax (828) 456-9298
Web site: www1.aksi.net/~cmark/balsm.htm

Hickory Haven Inn
361 Fiddlers' Lane/P. O. Box 88
Balsam, NC 28707
(800) 684-2836 (toll free), (828) 452-1106, Fax (828) 456-4830
Web site: www.primeline.com/~smkymtbb

Appalachian Cultural Center
"The Spirit of Appalachia" & "Heritage Alive"
371 Andy's Trout Farm Road
Otto, NC 28763 (about 50 miles from Waynesville and worth the drive)
Drama by playwright Amy Ammons Garza that tells the story of the Ammons family who helped settle the area. Heritage Alive uses music, story telling, and spontaneous visual art to depict the heritage and creativity of the Appalachian culture
(800) 711-0828 (toll free)

SILOHOUSE
VINEYARDS

*Cabernet
Sauvignon*

Vintage 1997
† **NORTH CAROLINA**
ALCOHOL 13.3% BY VOLUME 750ml

GROWN, PRODUCED & BOTTLED BY SILOHOUSE VINEYARDS
WAYNESVILLE, NORTH CAROLINA 28786

"Go thy way,
eat thy bread with joy,
and drink thy wine
with a merry heart;
for God now accepteth
thy works."
- Bible
Ecclesiastes 9. 7

South Carolina

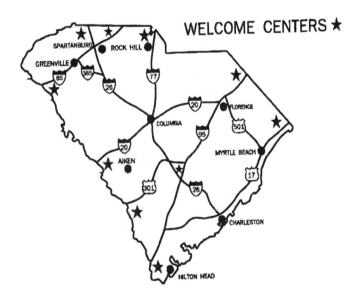

WELCOME CENTERS ★

South Carolina
Smiling Faces. Beautiful Places.

Cruse Vineyards & Winery

Kenneth and Susan Cruse
1683 Woods Road
Chester, South Carolina 29706
(803) 377-3944

Opening Hours: By appointment

About a mile and a half down a country road in the heart of the Olde English District lies one of South Carolina's best surprises. Cruse Vineyards & Winery nestles comfortably on 41 acres of gently rolling farmland with soil rich enough to grow succulent French-American hybrid and vinifera grapes. Grapes that each autumn become delicious, award winning wine.

It's a family affair for Kenneth and Susan Cruse and daughter Lauren. For more than ten years they have worked the land, endured the weather, fought the pests that threatened to destroy their crops, harvested the grapes and produced the wine. They built the winery and the barn themselves. They experimented with grape varieties and blends, originally making only very dry, oaky red wines. They soon found their customers wanted something lighter, so they changed their wines to suit their customers' tastes. Most of all, through the ups and downs, they've had fun.

"We made a pact in the beginning that when it wasn't fun anymore, we'd quit." explains Susan. More than ten years later, they're still growing grapes and making wine.

In the early 1980's Susan was in a high powered, high stress job. As daughter Lauren's primary years slipped away in day care, Susan decided she needed a career change. After much soul searching, she and Kenn decided to take their hobby of wine making and see if they could make a go of it commercially. Susan was interested in the farming side of the business, which got her outdoors, and gave her the opportunity to be home when daughter Lauren got out of school. With copies of renowned wine maker Phillip Wagner's books in hand, Susan quit her job. The couple cashed in their retirement and became vineyardists, planting their first 2 1/2 acres of grape vines in 1985. In March of 1988, they produced their first vintage and sold all 700 gallons by December. Today five acres of four Old World varieties produces, on the average, about 1100 gallons annually.

"It has been wildly successful. We have done far better making and selling wine than we first thought we would, but," Susan adds, "growing grapes is not for the fainthearted or the sissy. It requires a lot of knowledge, a lot of time, a lot of money and a lot of effort."

Pitfalls typical to all farming can be found in the grape and wine business says Susan. She has fought funguses that attack the vines, and birds and dear who love the ripening fruit She has raised registered Angus cattle for money to supplement the vineyard and thought of creative ways to market the wine. "The best way to make a million dollars," Susan laughs, "is to have five million and start a winery."

Every family member has a part in the business, especially during crush. A biochemist by training, Kenn likes the wine making process. He creates the blends and monitors the progress of each year's crop in his lab. Susan tends the vines and runs the harvest with five helpers. Lauren drives the tractor. Since the early varieties start ripening in August, picking begins around 6:30 a.m. so as to end around 11:30 a.m. when the day starts to really heat up.

During the winter, after fermentation and storage comes the bottling process. Susan says it usually takes the three of them twelve to fourteen hours to bottle one 540 gallon tank. That plus the labeling adds up to lots of family fun time. "They hate me by the time we're finished," laughs Susan.

Eighty five percent of the wine produced is sold at the winery. Varieties grown include Chardonnay, Vidal, Seyval, Chambourcin, and Melody. Winery tours are available by appointment and they periodically hold special events and tours for groups. Cruse Vineyards & Winery frequently teams up with The Inn at Merridun, located 29 miles away in Union, South Carolina and owned and operated by friends Jim and Peggy Waller. Special Wine Lovers' Weekends feature tasting classes and a tour of the vineyard. Once or twice a year the Merridun hosts gourmet meals featuring several courses each paired with a Cruse Vineyards wine.

The winery is open to the public 3:30 p.m. to 6:00 p.m. on Fridays and noon until 6:00 p.m. Saturdays, but it's best to call ahead if possible, especially for large groups. When you arrive, five wonderful wines await your pleasure. Says Susan, "This is what we do well, this is what we can do and what we like to do." And, yes, they're still having fun.

Directions to Cruse Vineyards & Winery

The short way with the dirt road.
Take Interstate 77 to the Chester exit (#65). Go west on SC 9 toward Chester for about 6 miles until you come to Cedarhurst Road on the right. There you'll see a red and while Cruse Vineyards sign. Turn right and go about one mile to Woods Road. Turn right on Woods and go about 6/10 of a mile to the gate and the Cruse Vineyards sign on your left. Note: Woods Road is a twisty dirt road.

The long way on the paved road.
Take Interstate 77 to the Chester exit (#65). Go west on SC 9 toward Chester for about 3 miles until you come to SC 909. Turn right and follow the road for 5 miles until you reach SC 72/SC 121 at the community of Lewis Turnout. Turn left and go about 1/2 mile to Hall Road and the green Cruse Vineyards sign on your left. Turn left and 7/10 of a mile to Woods Road. Turn right and go 1/2 mile to the gate and the Cruse Vineyards sign on your right.

Wine List

Proprietors White -a blend of Vidal, Seyval and Chardonnay (Chardonnay taste with a little more acid; not too dry and not too sweet)
Proprietors Blush - a blend of Chambourcin and chancellor (a fuller, drier flavor)
Seyval Blanc - a dry, white table wine with a crisp, smooth taste
Chambourcin - a full, ripe red, with a smooth finish

While You're Here

Cruse Vineyards lies in the north-central part of South Carolina's Olde English District. Here you'll find many place names taken directly from British towns and villages as well as a more English flavor to the Carolina lifestyle.

Olde English District Tourism Commission
P. O. Box 1440
Chester, SC 29706
(800) 968-5909 (toll free), (803) 789-7076, Fax (803) 789-7077
e-mail: sctravel@infoave.net
Web site: www.sctravel.net

Chester

Chester County Chamber of Commerce
109 Gadsden Street
Chester, SC 29706
(803) 581-4142, Fax (803) 581-2431

Chester County Historical Society Museum
McAliley Street
Local memorabilia and history housed in a 1914 jail. Free
(803) 385-2330

Chester State Park
State Road 72, 3 miles south west of Chester
Nature trail, camping, fishing, picnic areas and boat rentals.
(803) 385-2680

Bed & Breakfast Inns in Chester

Pinckney Inn
110 Pinckney Street
(803) 377-7466

York County

York County Convention & Visitors Bureau
201 E. Main Street/P. O. Box 11377
Rock Hill, SC 29731
(800) 866-5200 (toll free), (803) 329-5200, Fax (803) 329-0145
Web site: www.yccvb.com

A Revolutionary War "soldier" cooks his meal over an open fire during an historic re-enactment at Historic Brattonsville.

Historic Brattonsville
1444 Brattonsville Road
McConnells, SC 29726
10 miles west of Rock Hill off State Road 322
Restored plantation house, 19th century doctor's office and other historic architecture from 1750 to the 1930's.
(803) 684-2327

Paramount's Carowinds
13 miles north of Rock Hill off Interstate-77
Amuse yourself at this 100 acre theme park that stretches on both sides of the NC/SC state line. Rides, shows, water park and more.
(800) 888-4FUN (toll free for schedules), (803) 548-5300

Catawba Cultural Center
1536 Tom Steven Road (10 miles south east of Rock Hill)
Nature trail, exhibits and video about the Catawba Indian Nation. A craft store features distinctive Catawba pottery.
(803) 328-2427

Landsford Canal State historic Site
About 15 miles south of Rock Hill off U. S. Highway 21
Features the remains of the 1820's canal system designed by Robert Mills. Museum, interpretive center, nature trails, fishing, playground, picnic area
(803) 789-5800

Andrew Jackson State Park
198 Andrew Jackson Park Rd. (9 miles north of Lancaster on U. S. 521)
"Old Hickory", America's 7th president was born near here. A museum and one-room school depict that pioneer era. Camping, fishing, nature trail, picnic area.
(803) 285-3344

Rock Hill

Rock Hill Area Chamber of Commerce
115 Dave Lyle Blvd./P. O. Box 590
Rock Hill, SC 29730/29731
(803) 324-7500, Fax (803) 324-1889

Glencairn Gardens
Charlotte & Edgemont Avenues
Stroll through 7.6 acres of sculpted terraces and flower beds. Reflecting pool and fountain. Free
(803) 329-5540

Bed & Breakfast Inns in Rock Hill

Book & Spindle B&B
626 Oakland Avenue
Rock Hill, SC 29730
(803) 328-1913

Park Avenue Inn
347 Park Avenue
Rock Hill, SC 29730
(803) 325-1764, Fax (803) 325-1764

East Main Guest House
600 East Main Street
Rock Hill, SC 29730
(803) 366-1161
Web site: www.bbonline.com/sc/eastmain/

York

Museum of York County
4621 Mt. Gallant Road
York, SC 29732-9905

Native American crafts and customs are exhibited at the Catawba Cultural Center

More than 200 animal exhibits from all over the world, Native American artifacts, planetarium, three art galleries, nature trail and museum store. (803) 329-2121, Fax (803) 329-5249

Windy Hill Orchard & Cider Mill
1860 Hwy. 5
York, SC 29745
Educational farm tours, hay rides and cider making. Fresh baked apple pies, and cider made the olde English way. The southern most "cidery" in America. Individuals and groups welcome.
(803) 684-0690

Union County - Union
Union County Chamber of Commerce
135 W. Maine Street
Union, SC 29379
(864) 427-9039, Fax (864) 427-9030

Union County Museum
2nd floor of the American Federal Building, Main Street
Displays memorabilia of area history, including Union's first fire engine, muzzle loading 18th Century rifles, Confederate uniforms and more. Operated by the Union County Historical Foundation
(864) 427-7950 Mike Becknell, or (864) 427-2578 Dr. Allan Charles

Bed & Breakfast Inns in Union

The Inn at Merridun
100 Merridun Place
Union, SC 29379
(888) 892-6020 (toll free), (864) 427-7052, Fax (864) 429-0373
email: merridun@carol.net
Web site: www.bbonline.com/sc/merridun/

Juxa Plantation
117 Wilson Road
(864) 427-8688
Pets welcome
Web site: www.bbonline.com/sc/juxa/index.html
        and www.virtualcities.com

"And Noah he often said to his wife
when he sat down to dine,
'I don't care where the water goes if
it doesn't get into the wine.'"
- G. K. Chesterton
Wine and Water

Grown, Produced and Bottled
by Montmorenci Vineyards
2989 Charleston Hwy.
Aiken, South Carolina 29801
(803) 649-4870

Montmorenci Vineyards

Bob and Elaine Scott
2989 Charleston Highway
Aiken, South Carolina   29801
(803) 649-4870

Opening Hours:
Wednesday - Saturday 10:00 a.m. to 6:00 p.m.
Closed on Major Holidays and
During the First Two Weeks of January

What do peanuts and grapes have in common? They're both grown by Bob Scott near Aiken, South Carolina. Now which ones do you suppose he makes into wine?

Bob Scott, Sr. is a chemist, research scientist, peanut farmer, vine-yardist and vintner rolled into one. Son, Bob Scott, Jr. is following in his dad's footsteps. The family has been very successfully growing peanuts in the village of Montmorenci, east of Aiken, since 1970. In the late 1980's, they decided to add another crop.

"We started the vines as a lark," Bob explains. "It was something we were interested in trying, to see if French and American hybrid grapes would grow this far south and at this low an elevation. You see, we're only about 490 feet above sea level here. A lot of people thought we couldn't do it, but, we started reading everything we could get our hands on, and working with the university, trying to see what would work."

The Scotts planted their first 100 vines of Arkansas table grapes in 1987, but drought and the vines' susceptibility to disease took their toll. The crop ended in disaster. The next year they tried again with some other varieties. They planted a few vines each of Chambourcin, Cayuga, Chardonnay and Seyval. It wasn't an instant success, but the vines did take hold and began producing grapes. Some of those vines are still producing today. In all, the Scotts have experimented with over 88 varieties of French and American hybrids. After much trial and error, lots of hard work and years of experimenting, Montmorenci Vineyards knows what does and doesn't work.

Today, Bob and his winemaker Bob, Jr. release about a dozen varietals and blends each year, from grapes grown on about 20 acres of vineyards. Current varieties include Chambourcin, Suwanee, Cayuga, Melody, Vignoles, and Blanc du Bois. They also grow a number of experimental vines in conjunction with the University of South Carolina, Clemson for research purposes. Such varieties as Cabernet Sauvignon, Shiraz, Merlot, and Traminette have had low to moderate success, some being susceptible to disease and vine rot. The research has helped the USC agricultural program to know what varieties can be successfully grown in South Carolina, and helped Bob know which ones make good wine. The Montmorenci philosophy is "only the best wines from the best grapes." Period!

As for the wines, winemaker Bob Scott, Jr. has had a lot of success in experimenting as well. Many of his varieties and blends have won medals from the American Wine Society, and such shows as the Atlanta Wine Summit, the Springfest Wine Festival at Hilton Head Island, and the International Eastern Wine Competition. That's a long way from his family's basement where he made his first batch of wine.

"Grand-daddy always kept a crock," says Bob, Jr. "One time I asked him what that was and he said that was where he was making his wine. He had some Muscadines growing over at his place so one day I went out and picked a small gallon bucket of 'em and took 'em home. I got in my mom's cook book and found a recipe in there for wine, and made some wine in a quart jar. I guess I was about 12 at the time." Bob doesn't remember if the wine was any good or not, but it was his first batch of wine.

Due to Montmorenci's climate and elevation, some of their wines have a more mature flavor than is produced at other places. For instance, in New York, home of the Cayuga grape, the wine tends to be a bit more acidic. With lower free acid going into fermentation, Montmorenci's Cayuga has less of a bite.

Bob Scott still primarily grows peanuts, about one and a half million pounds of them a year, but he loves the vines and the wines. He produces about 5000 cases annually. "There is a character about the wine that's raised here," he says. "We definitely have our own flavor."

Directions to Montmorenci Vineyards

From Interstate 20, take either Aiken exit (U.S. Highway 1 or State Road 19) and go about 5 to 7 miles to downtown Aiken. From there take U. S. Highway 78 east about 5 miles to the village of Montmorenci. Look for the vines and the Tudor-style tasting room. Montmorenci Vineyards is on your left.

From Interstate 95, take Exit 77 to U. S. Highway 78. Travel west on Highway 78 for about 70 miles to the village of Montmorenci. Montmorenci Vineyards is on your right. Look for the vines and the Tudor-style tasting room.

Wine List

White Wines

Savannah White - a light white wine made from the Cayuga grape; mild but bone dry; tickles that palate with a slight effervescence; serve chilled (55 degrees); very drinkable for many occasions.

Melody - a crisp dry white wine with hints of citrus and peach flavors; well balanced acidity; serve slightly chilled (60 degrees); fine with chicken and light meats.

de Caradeuc White - named for the French Canadian founder of the village of Montmorenci, this wine is an Alsatian style white wine with floral and apple notes; it is a blend of Cayuga, Melody, Blanc du Bois and Suwanee; served chilled (55 degrees) before or with meals.

Seyval - a rich white wine aged in French and American oak barrels; serve this White Burgundy style wine at almost room temperature (65 degrees).

Blanc du Bois - an intensely perfumed

and flavored dry white wine that is recollective of the Tropics; followed by rich and lingering flavors; serve slightly chilled (60 degrees) with strongly flavored foods.

Suwanee - a semi-sweet white wine with a bold Southern bouquet and a delicate varietal character; serve slightly chilled (60 degrees) on any occasion.

Vin Eclipser - a late harvest dessert wine reminiscent of apricot and honeyed fruit flavors; great alone, or with most any dessert; serve slightly chilled (60 degrees).

Red Wines
de Caradeuc Red - a medium bodied red wine, laced with currant and nutmeg that's aromatically pleasing; easy to warm up to; serve at almost room temperature (65 degrees).

Barrel Fermented Rosé - a medium bodied wine with French oak, vanilla, and black cherry aromas that spiral into integrated berry flavors; serve slightly chilled (60 degrees).

Chambourcin - a big, ripe and generous red wine that spends two years in French and American oak, with a wonderful harmony of flavor, hinting of cedar, spice and smoke against a solid backdrop of cherry and tobacco; beautifully proportioned, with fine tannins to ensure cellar worthiness; serve at room temperature (70 degrees).

Rosé - an immediately attractive wine that's soft, slightly sweet with plum flavors and rose petal aromas; serve slightly chilled (60 degrees).

Triple Crown Blush - a light and fruity blush wine made from our Cayuga, Suwanee and Chambourcin grapes; serve chilled before or with meals (55 degrees).

Sparkling Wines
Brut - a special dosage created this complex sparkling wine with racy flavors of pear and spice followed by a subtleness of toast that explodes into a creamy floral finish. Our Brut is made in the traditional French *Methode Champenoise.*

Suggestions for Pairing Wine With Food from Montmorenci Vineyards

Wine is best enjoyed with food and can actually enhance the flavor of your meal. This is known as the marriage of wine and food. In order for this union to work, you must know the taste of the wine and the taste of the dish. Then you have to imagine how the match will succeed. To make things easier, we've listed some of our favorite matches. We all have different taste preferences, so don't be afraid to experiment with wine and food. Bon appetite.

Lamb - Blanc du Bois, with its intense flavors, is an excellent choice for the gamey flavor of lamb. Seyval, with all its richness, is a delicious flavor partner as well. If you prefer a red wine, Chambourcin will please the palate.

Pork - de Caradeuc Red, with its medium bodied wine characteristics, provides a savory addition to stuffed chops, grilled ribs, or smoked ham. A fine mate for baked or glazed ham is Rosé.

Poultry - Seyval, with its smoky oak flavor, tastes great with turkey, chicken, Cornish hen, quail, pheasant, or duck. For delicate poultry dishes, try Suwanee, Melody, Savannah White or Brut. Barrel Fermented Rosé or Chambourcin can enhance the flavor of smoked turkey or smoked duck.

Beef - Chambourcin provides a full-bodied accompaniment to all beef dishes. For those preferring a lighter red wine, Barrel Fermented Rosé makes a delectable combination with beef.

Fish - Savannah White, with its lightness and dryness, enhances almost any delicate fish or simply prepared shellfish. Seyval, full-flavored and dry, is a complement to fishes such as grouper, flounder, or swordfish. Blanc du Bois, with its complex and intense flavors, pairs well with crayfish, jambalaya, and strongly-flavored fishes such as salmon, tuna, shark, or mahi-mahi.

Dessert - Brut, a racy sparkling wine, is marvelous with key lime pie. For cheesecake lovers, Vin Eclipser is the perfect accompaniment. Suwanee, with its Southern bouquet, is a harmonious choice for fresh fruit. Dark chocolate and Chambourcin make an extraordinary match.

While You're Here

Montmorenci Vineyards lies in the heart of South Carolina's Thoroughbred Country. Just after the Revolutionary War, this four county area, with its mild winters and year round green pastures, was found to be ideal for raising horses. Today it is known the world over as an equestrian training center that produces champions. It has also been a wintering wonderland for the wealthy. Besides horse and rider heaven, once a year the whole place goes golf ga-ga as it takes part in neighboring Augusta, Georgia's grand golf event, the Masters. There's a lot to see and do here, so jump in.

Aiken County
Thoroughbred Country
2748 Wagener Road/P. O. Box 850
Aiken, SC 29801/29802
(803) 649-7981, Fax (803) 649-2248
e-mail: tbredco@scescape.net
Web site: www.scescape.net/~lscog/depart/tbredco.htm

Bed & Breakfast Inns in Montmorenci

Annie's Inn Bed & Breakfast
3083 Charleston Highway
Montmorenci, SC 29839
(803) 649-6836, Fax (803) 642-6709

Aiken
Aiken Chamber of Commerce
121 Richland Avenue East
Aiken, SC 29801
(800) 542-4536 (toll free), (803) 641-1111, Fax (803) 641-4174
Web site: www.chamber.aiken.net

DuPont Planetarium
University of South Carolina - Aiken
45-seat planetarium, projects over 9,000 stars and simulates 3-dimensional space travel
Reservations required
(803) 641-3654

*The Aiken County Historical Museum, housed in Banksia,
a 1930's Winter Colony mansion, has over 30 rooms of exhibits.*

Hopeland Gardens & Thoroughbred Hall of Fame
Corner of Whiskey Road & Dupree Place
14-acre park and gardens includes a touch and scent trail and a museum. Features the champions of thoroughbred flatracers and steeplechase horses which were trained in Aiken from 1942 to today. Photographs, trophies, racing silks, memorabilia.
(803) 642-7630

Aiken County Historical Museum
433 Newberry Street SW
Aiken, SC 29801
Housed in a 1930's Winter Colony mansion, the museum has 30 rooms of exhibits. Also has 1808 log cabin and 1890 one room school house on grounds.
(803) 642-2015 or (803) 642-2017, Fax (803) 642-2016

Aiken Center for the Arts
122 Laurens Street
Aiken, SC 29801
Gallery exhibits of local, state and regional artists. Art shows and instruction.
(803) 641-9094

Hitchcock Woods
Center of Aiken
Largest urban forest in the country. 2000 acres features trails for hiking and horseback riding. No motorized vehicles permitted.

Aiken State Park
1145 State Park Road (16 miles east of Aiken on State Road 302)
Windsor, SC 29856
Second oldest state park in South Carolina, built in 1934. Canoe rentals, fishing, hiking and overnight camping.
(803) 649-2857

Bed & Breakfast Inns in Aiken

The Briar Patch
544 Magnolia Lane SE
Aiken, SC 29801
National Register of Historic Places
(803) 649-2010

Brodie Residence
422 York Street SE
Aiken, SC 29801
(803) 648-1445

Town & Country Inn
2340 Sizemore Circle
Aiken, SC 29803
Includes stable for visitors with horses
(803) 642-0270, Fax (803) 642-1299
e-mail: tcinn@aol.com
Web site: www.bbonline.com/sc/towncountry

Interesting Eats in Aiken

A'La Carte Gourmet & Cafe/Linda's Bistro
210 The Alley
Aiken, SC 29801
(803) 648-4853

Aiken Brewing Company (Brew Pub)
140 Laurens Street SW
Aiken, SC 29801
(803) 502-0707

Acropolis Pizza
1647 Richland Avenue
Aiken, SC 29801
(803) 649-7601

Mango's Tropical Cafe
149 Laurens Street SW
Aiken, SC 29801
(803) 643-0620

Westside Bowery
151 Bee Lane
Aiken, SC 29801
(803) 648-2900

NO. 10 Downing Street
241 Laurens Street SW
Aiken, SC 29801
(803) 642-9062

Wine Shops in Aiken

Palmetto Package Shops
230 Park avenue
Aiken, SC 29801
(803) 649-6961

North Augusta
Greater North Augusta Chamber of Commerce
235 Georgia Avenue
North Augusta, SC 29841
(803) 279-2323, Fax (803) 279-0003

Living History Park
Corner of Lake Avenue & West Spring Grove Avenue
8-acre downtown park features birds and flowing stream

Redcliffe State Historic Site
181 Redcliffe Road (about 7 miles south east of North Augusta off U.S. Highway 278)
Beach Island, SC 29842
1850's home of Governor James Henry Hammond. Outbuildings and grounds, hiking, fishing and picnicking.
(803) 827-1473

Bed & Breakfast Inns in North Augusta

Rosemary Hall & Lookaway Hall
804 Carolina Avenue
North Augusta, SC 29841
National Register of Historic Places
(800) 531-5578 (toll free), (803) 278-6222, Fax (803) 278-4877

South Carolina's Thoroughbred Country is known throughout the world as an equestrian training center claiming many National Champions.

Barnwell County

Barnwell County Chamber of Commerce
P. O. Box 898
Barnwell, SC 29812
(803) 259-7446, Fax (803) 259-0030

Blackville

Barnwell State Park
3 miles south of Blackville on State Road 3
307 acres, nature trail, cabins, camping, picnicking and swimming
(803) 284-2212

Bed & Breakfast Inns in Blackville

Floyd Manor Inn
111 Dexter Street
Blackville, SC 29817
(800) 321-1759 (toll free), (803) 284-3736

Grandpa's Cabin
322 Main Street
Blackville, SC 29817
(803) 284-3117

Interesting Eats in Blackville

Miller's Bread Basket
322 Main Street
Blackville, SC 29817
(803) 284-3117

Interesting Eats in Barnwell County

Ballard's Cafe
1618 Main Street
Barnwell, SC 29812
(803) 259-1245

Barnwell

Barnwell County Museum
Marlboro Avenue
A collection of local memorabilia and history. Free
(803) 259-1916

Barnwell Sundial
Courthouse Square
Rare, vertical sundial has given the correct time of day for over 150 years.
Only one of its kind in the country.

Church of the Holy Apostles & Rectory
Hagood Avenue At Burr Street
Built in 1856, the church is on the National Historic Register. Occupied by
Union soldiers during the Civil War. The large stone baptismal font is be-
lieved to date from medieval times. Free

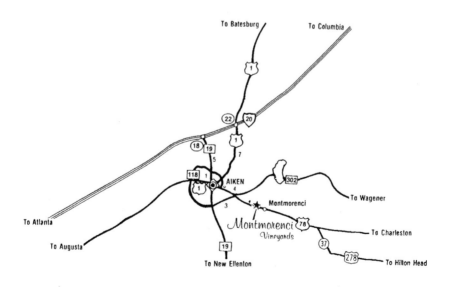

Wineries To Be

Wineries To Be in North Carolina

J. Berrie Brown Vineyards

If all "grows" well, says Sandi Ford, partner in the new J. Berrie Brown Vineyards, the 1999 harvest will include Chardonnay, Merlot, Chambourcin, Seyval Blanc, and Cabernet Sauvignon. The vineyards are located on State Road 98 off U. S. Highway 1, North near Louisburg.

Sisters June Bayman (left) and Vicki Weigle (right) inspect their grape crop at La Belle Amie Vineyards.

La Belle Amie Vineyard and Winery

Vicki Weigle & June and Brad Bayman
11050 Highway 90 West
Little River, South Carolina 29566
(843) 399-WINE (9463)

Opening planned for early 1999
Call for information

Not far from the golf and glitz of South Carolina's Grand Strand, grape vines grow serenely on a former tobacco farm. Surrounded by the quiet of the countryside and nourished by a multitude of "angels," La Belle Amie Vineyard could well be in the south of France instead of just two miles from the packed traffic lanes of U. S. Highway 17. Sisters Vicki Weigle and June Bayman are hoping that will be just the draw for visitors to their vineyard and winery.

"We want to create a country ambiance so visitors will feel like they're on a farm in the South, which they are." says Vicki. The farm is the home and birthplace of Vicki and June's mother Berta Bellamy Weigle.

The sisters chose the name La Belle Amie to honor their mother. It means "The Beautiful Friend" in French and is the origin of the surname Bellamy.

Guests will arrive on a winding road that will pass the first vineyard and continue through a strand of old hardwood trees leading up to the winery. The winery will set on a hill next to a pond formed aeons ago by a meteorite and surrounded by cypress trees dripping with Spanish moss.

Will is the operative word, for at the moment, plans are still on paper, but Vicki hopes that won't be for long. With the help of her "angels," La Belle Amie Vineyard will soon be a reality.

In 1993, Vicki wasn't looking to trade in her corporate suits for blue jeans. As Director of Catering and Convention Services at the Westin Hotel in Houston, Texas, Vicki planned and coordinated events for Houston society. "My friends never saw me in a pair of jeans," laughs Vicki. "They still can't imagine I'm doing this."

Vicki's mother, then 86, was living with June and her family in Charlotte, North Carolina. She had gone there after being attacked at the farm by a Pit Bull Terrier. The sisters didn't feel comfortable leaving her alone, but after a while the draw of home was too much. Mrs. Weigle wanted to return to the farm, so Vicki decided to quit her job and move to there with her.

"I knew I couldn't just retire," says Vicki. "If I took a hotel or event planning job, I wouldn't be home for Mother, so I started thinking, what could I do here?" A lot of thoughts started swirling around in her head. How could she use her corporate sales skills and knowledge of catering and event planning? The 100 year old grape vines near the house were a clue. She recalled that her uncle used to make wine using an old Horry County recipe that would "knock you flat." Then it came to her; she could grow grapes, make wine and open a winery.

What a great idea! It seemed simple enough. Clear the land, plant vines, pick the grapes, make the wine, and the customers will come. The reality was another matter.

Vicki started reading and researching and learned that the vines had to be planted at a certain time, not just whenever she was ready. She lost the first planting season. Then she learned that before she could plant the vines, or even prepare the land, she had to clear the trees out of the fields. "I called every tree service in the yellow pages. No one would even come and give me an estimate. I found out later what I needed was a bull dozer to clear it out. I was about to lose the second planting season when my first angel came along."

Vicki was in the local hardware store when someone mentioned a name of someone she had known years before when she used to spend her summers on the farm. She casually asked what he was doing now and learned that he operated a landscaping service. "I called him and told him who I was. He didn't remember me, but said he'd be glad to come out and have a look at the property. When he got here, he said, 'Oh, yes, I remember you.' Two days later all the trees were gone and the field leveled. If it weren't for Donnie, this vineyard would not be here."

After that things began falling into place and angels just seemed to appear when needed. June and her husband Brad Bayman, a pilot with U. S. Airways decided to move to the area in order to help with Mrs. Weigle and the vineyard. June is the Manager of Retail Sales and Merchandising while Brad manages the vineyard and winery operations. There have been offers of help in areas from financial planning to vine pruning. In 1997, friends came from all over the world to help with the first harvest. Vicki promised them a party afterward, but disaster struck when Mrs. Weigle fell and broke her hip. Vicki spent the rest of the day at the hospital, but the grapes were harvested. She says she owes them the party, and more.

Recently a man was driving by, spotted the vineyard and pulled in to talk to Vicki. Turns out he's is retired wine maker who is interested is La Bell Amie's concept and has offered to help. Another angel in the making?

"Donnie, Hazel, June, Brad, Chuck, Bob, all the friends who came to the harvest; I don't know what I would have done without all those angels!" exclaims Vicki. "What other business could you start and have all those people want to help you."

La Belle Amie Vineyard currently has two acres of Carlos and Noble grapes planted, about 460 vines. "We wanted something that we were sure would grow here, so NC State suggested the Carlos and Noble." says Vicki. They will produce wine from the Muscadine grapes, but they also have other plans. Recently, Vicki went to France to negotiate a deal for La Belle Amie Vineyard.

"We are working with several vineyards in the Languedoc region in the south of France." explains Vicki. "They are going to bottle a selection of wines (Cabernet, Chardonnay and Merlot) for us under our label which we will sell in the gift shop and winery, so it is important to note that most of La Belle Amie's wine will be imported from France. We also plan to experiment with growing some French-American hybrids of our own. The climate of Languedoc is similar to our area, so we're going to try planting Cynthiana, Blanc du Bois and a French grape called Picpoul. This way, no matter what happens, poor harvest, bad weather, whatever, we'll have a continual supply of wine."

Vicki says she found it ironic that during her stay in France, she met Bellamys in the region where she purchased her wines. "They said, 'Oh, Vik-kee. Maybe we are related."

Except for summers spent as a child and young adult, this is the first time Vicki has lived on the farm. "I didn't grow up on the farm, but I think I always had farming in my soul." she says. "At my condominium in Houston I badgered the grounds keepers into giving me a little plot of land to grow roses. I've always liked working with the soil. There's such wonderful satisfaction in growing things."

Planting probably does come naturally to Vicki. She is the great, great, great, granddaughter of North Carolina planter Dr. John D. Bellamy, whose city residence, the Bellamy Mansion built between 1859 and 1861, is located on Market Street in Wilmington,

With the help of Odie the "vineyard dog," Vicki Inspects the vineyards and cruises the grounds in a golf cart.

North Carolina. Vicki says she plans to tie that in with her marketing of the vineyard.

She is also interested in promoting the connection of wines and foods and wine and health. "In the French way, you don't just have a meal, you dine. You have several courses over the evening. It's relaxing and fun."

With the help of her angels, Vicki sees La Belle Amie Vineyard becoming a unique attraction on the Grand Strand. In an area noted for having over 100 golf courses, tee shirt shops by the dozens and bumper cars both off and on the roadways, La Belle Amie Vineyard will offer a quiet spot to relax and listen to the sounds of the country.

Directions
From Little River, take U. S. Highway 17 to State Road 90. Go about two miles west. The vineyard is on your left.

While You're Here

Golf, beaches, shopping, nightlife, attractions, sun, surf and sand all describe the incomparable Myrtle Beach area. With over 100 golf courses, outlet malls, and miles of beaches, the Grand Strand is - well - Grand! This is a vacation wonderland, so dive in.

Horry County, South Carolina
Little River
Little River Chamber of Commerce
P. O. Box 400
Little River, SC 29566
(843) 249-6604
Web site: http://home1.gte.net/lrcoc/index.html

Myrtle Beach
Myrtle Beach Area Convention Bureau
1200 N. Oak Street/P. O. Box 2115
Myrtle Beach, SC 29578
(800) 488-8998 (toll free), (843) 448-1629, Fax (843) 448-3010
Web site: www.myrtlebeachlive.com

Alligator Adventure
U. S. Highway 17 at Barefoot Landing
Research institute offers live shows and demonstrations. Rare alligators and crocodiles, snakes and other exotic wildlife.
(800) 631-0789 (toll free), (843) 361-0789

Franklin G. Burroughs - Simeon B. Chapin Art Museum
3100 S. Ocean Blvd.
Myrtle Beach, SC 29577
The 1920's beach house of Col. Elliott White Springs now features rotating art exhibits, a gift shop and tea room.
(843) 238-2510

Ripley's Aquarium
29th Avenue N & 17 Bypass at Broadway at the Beach
Journey through the world's longest underwater acrylic tunnel with a moving walkway, surrounded by sharks, moray eels and colorful reef fish. Touch the winged inhabitants of Ray Bay. $36 million aquatic collection.
(843) 916-0888

Bed & Breakfast Inns in Myrtle Beach

Brustman House
400 25ᵗʰ Avenue South
Myrtle Beach, SC 29577
English style afternoon teas served
(800) 448-7699 (toll free), (843) 448-7699, Fax (843) 626-2478
Web site: www.gatewaymediaworks.com/brustmanhouse

Cain House B&B
206 29ᵗʰ Avenue South
Myrtle Beach, SC 29577
(843) 448-3063

Conway
Conway Area Chamber of Commerce
203 Main Street/P. O. Box 831
Conway, SC 29528
(843) 248-2273, Fax (843) 248-0003
Web site: www.conwaysc.org

Horry County Museum
438 Main Street
Conway, SC 29526
Pronounced O-ree, Horry County has a rich history rooted in the plantation era. Archaeological and historic exhibits in an old post office building.
(843) 248-1542, Fax (843) 248-1854

Ocean Isle Beach, North Carolina
Museum of Coastal Carolina
21 East 2ⁿᵈ Street
Ocean Isle Beach, NC 28469
Museum of natural history focusing on the coastal region of the Carolinas.
Large dioramas of freshwater wetland, salt marsh and ocean reef. Shell collection has every native species. Native American artifacts, tide and solar
exhibits and antique fishing equipment. Gift shop.
(910) 579-1016, Fax (910) 579-1016

Bed & Breakfast Inns in Ocean Isle Beach
Goose Creek Bed & Breakfast
1901 Egret Street SW
Ocean Isle Beach, NC 28469 *(cont. next page)*

(800) 275-6540 (toll free), (910) 754-5849, Fax (910) 754-5849
e-mail: weblync@infoave.net
Web site: www.weblync.com/goose_creek

Bed & Breakfast Inns in Shallotte, NC

Breakfast Creek Bed & Breakfast
4361 Ocean Breeze Avenue SW
Shallote, NC 28470
(888) 754-3614 (toll free), (910) 754-3614

A one hundred year old grape vine grows at La Belle Amie Vineyards.

"Fill ev'ry glass, for wine inspires us,
And fires us
With courage, love and joy."
- John Gay
The Beggar's Opera

Truluck Vineyards

Jay and Wendy Truluck
701 Truluck Vineyards Road
Lake City, South Carolina 29560
(843) 389-0100, Fax (843) 389-0103

First vintage expected fall of 1999
Call for information

Mention the name Truluck Vineyards in South Carolina and you'll probably jog a memory or two. One person thinks it's long gone. Another thinks it's still there. Both are right. More than ten years after it's last award winning vintage, Truluck Vineyards is the oldest new winery in the Carolinas.

Originally opened in 1976 by Dr. James P. Truluck, Truluck Vineyards was the first commercial winery in South Carolina and the first in the south to produce wines from French vinifera and American hybrid grapes. Located near Lake City in the South Carolina Pee Dee region, it was originally believed that only the native Muscadine grapes could grow there. Not only did the European varieties grow, but the wines they made won over 25 medals in competitions during the next 11 years, including Best of

Show in the 1984 Atlanta International Wine Festival. Now, more than 22 years later, Dr. Truluck's son Jay is reopening the vineyards and winery with plans to restore them to their former glory, and beyond.

The Truluck story goes back to France in the late 1950's when Dr. James was stationed with the Air Force in the Loire Valley. He saw similarities between the region and his home in South Carolina and thought why not try growing grapes there. Jay's birth was expected soon and rather than have her son born a French citizen, Jay's mother elected to come back to the U. S. and have her baby at home. Even so, Jay was born on July 14th, Bastille Day.

"I always thought it might have been neat to have been born a dual citizen in this line of work," laughs Jay, who was 11 years old when he helped his father plant the first grape vines in 1971. Jay grew up in the vineyards, first planting and tending the vines, then making wines and managing the growing business. He studied oenology at UC-Davis and Mississippi State. By the mid-1980's, production was up to 15,000 gallons annually.

"My father and I were constantly arguing about the size of the vineyard because I was the one who had to maintain it and care for it. There were 52 miles of vines." says Jay. "My mother died in 1981 and the two of us had kind of balanced my father out because she had been a partner in the winery. After she died, it was kind of like, this was his show."

Jay left the vineyards in 1987 and began working for Santee Cooper at Myrtle Beach, but the vineyards never left him. In 1994, Jay returned to Lake City and bought the family farm out of foreclosure. "I had a great job with the state on the Beach, but I decided that if I didn't come up here and try this, it would haunt me 'till the day I died."

Because he planted all of the original vines, Jay knew just what varieties were growing where. He pulled up all 75 acres of vines and re-planted. He now has eight acres and plans to keep the vineyard that size, concentrating on Chardonnay, Cabernet Sauvignon, Cabernet Franc, Merlot and Chambourcin. Much of the Chambourcin has been propagated from the original vines by cutting all the trunks back and leaving the root.

"It's hard to say how long they've been in the ground. Some of my vines are four years old going on 30.I haven't been able to find anyone who can answer the question. Will the vines come across as four years old or 30 years old." He says his experimental wine doesn't come across as a four year old.

One major change in the new Truluck vintages will be immediately apparent. With the increase in red wine consumption in the 1990's, Jay plans to produce his Chambourcin as a varietal. "Chambourcin was one of our mainstays in the '80's, but unfortunately at that point in time, there was no red wine boom like we're experiencing now. We had to find alternatives for it, so we made it into both a blush and a rosé. I've got a lot of Chambourcin planted now but I don't plan to blush a bit of it."

Jay is taking his time, letting his vines mature and not rushing things. He says he knows what the land is capable of producing, but he's not ready yet to start making wine. Refurbishing the old French-Provincial style tasting room and winery (with underground cellars) and cleaning up the property has been time consuming. He has single handedly planted and tended the vines, and created a lovely ante-bellum live oak avenue at the entrance to the vineyards. He has built fences, a new house and a horse barn. A new feature of Truluck Vineyards is the addition of an equestrian center, wife Wendy's dream. Riding lessons, trail rides and boarding go hand in hand with plans to host horse shows.

"What better thing to bring to a winery than an equestrian event!" declares Jay. "That's what she's always wanted to do and I've always wanted to do this, so as long as we can take both of our things we've always wanted to do and put them together and make a living out of them, then we'll be happy."

Asked if he thinks he'll be successful in reopening Truluck Vineyards, Jay replies, "What is success? Making a lot of money? We weren't financially successful the first time, but we produced wines that were capable of competing with anybody else in the world. If you view it from that standpoint, then that's success."

Directions
From Lake City, take State Road 341 east to McCutcheon Road. Turn right and go 2 1/2 miles to Truluck Vineyards Road and take a right into the vineyards.

The author and Jay Truluck are dwarfed by an 18 year old wild grape vine.

While You're Here

As every South Carolina school child knows, this area is the Pee Dee, home of the mighty river that winds its way to the Atlantic at Winyah Bay. The river was named for its native people and today this rich agricultural region abounds in museums and state parks.

Florence County
Greater Lake City Chamber of Commerce
144 South Acline Street/P. O. Box 669
Lake City, SC 29560
(843) 394-8611
Web site: www.lakecitysc.com

Florence Convention & Visitors Bureau
(843) 664-0330, Fax (843) 665-9580
Web site: www.pdtourism.com

Lake City
Browntown Museum
SC 341, 9 miles east of Lake City
A classic old farmstead, including the Brown-Burrows House, built around 1835. Cotton gin, corn crib, smokehouse and outhouse. Groups, call for special opening times.
(843) 558-2355

Moore Memorial Museum
111 Singletary Avenue
Lake City, SC 29554
Changing exhibits in a renovated 1920's house, featuring a children's room, art room, exhibit on all 84 South Carolina governors and other collectibles.

Lynches River State Park
12 miles north of Lake City, off Highway 52
Relaxing woodland retreat offering river fishing, bird watching, picnicking and pool swimming.
(843) 389-2785

Woods Bay State Natural Area
Off U. S. Highway 301 12 miles west of Lake City
Natural formations called Carolina Bays are shallow geologic dishes of un-

known origin. Boardwalk through the wetlands allows for bird watching and alligator gazing, canoeing and picnicking.
(843) 659-4445

Williamsburg County
The Williamsburg County Chamber of Commerce
130 E. Main Street/P. O. Box 696
Kingstree, SC 29556
(843) 354-6431
e-mail: khmtown@ftc-i.net

Kingstree
Thorntree
SC 527
Built in 1749 by James Witherspoon, this is thought to be the oldest house in the Pee Dee area.
(843) 354-6431

Williamsburg County Art Gallery
108 W. Main Street
Kingstree, SC 29556
Victorian era building features revolving art exhibits
(843) 354-7247

Williamsburg County Museum
Main and Academy Streets
Historic archives including early maps and a dug-out canoe.
(843) 354-6431

Even though a number of people have tried, no one has yet found a way to drink for a living.
- Jean Kerr (b. 1923)
U.S. author, playwright
Sydney, in Poor Richard, act 1.

Crescent Mountain Vineyards

Ray and Lucille Stamm
10 Road of Vines
Travelers Rest, SC 29690
(877) 836-VINE (toll free), (864) 836-VINE (8463)

Opening planned for Fall 1999
Call for information

Stroll along the Rue des Vignes and drink in the fragrance of the vines growing heavy with succulent old world varietal grapes. Shop for antiques and collectibles in the village, or buy baguettes in the patisserie. Lounge in a cafe and drink coffee or sip a glass of local wine in the ancient winery overlooking the châteaux that dot the hillside. What's your hurry? Relax, after all, this is - South Carolina?

Yes! Through the vision of developer Ray Stamm and his wife Lucille, and the magic of builder Mike Wallis, a small part of France is appearing in the heart of the Cherokee Foothills in South Carolina's Upcountry. The Village at Crescent Mountain Vineyards sits on 140 rolling acres of land and overlooks a misty blue hill, with the fabled Blue Ridge Mountains rising behind it. Located 20 miles north of Greenville, South Carolina, and 44 miles south of Asheville, North Carolina, the Village at Crescent Mountain Vineyards plans to be a destination for weary and thirsty mountain travelers.

In 1996, Ray and Lucille Stamm decided to bring their love of the French countryside to South Carolina. They started planting grape vines, first Cabernet Sauvignon, then Cabernet Franc, Seyval Blanc and Vidal Blanc. 1998 saw the first Chardonnay vines planted. Today, 21 acres of vines grace the hillside in three, neat plots. Eventually, the goal is to have 40 to 50 acres of several different varieties.

"This area in northwestern South Carolina is very similar in climate and altitude to the Provençe region of France," Ray explains. "We've been working with the agriculture department at Clemson University to see what varieties will grow best. We're also experimenting with wines, and plan to release our first vintage in the fall of 1999." Production plans call for about 10,000 cases annually.

Currently under construction is the 14 room French country inn that is the focal point of the village. The winery and tasting room will sit atop man-made caves that will duplicate the look and conditions of ancient French wine cellars. Ray is looking for an old barn to move on site and convert into the winery, just as many old barns are used in France today. "Winsboro Blue" granite lines the hillsides creating stone fences, and other reusable building materials will give the village that old world look.

Plans for activities include winery tours, wine tastings, outdoor concerts in a hillside amphitheater and special events year round, such as the Annual Dividing Waters Omni Bicycle Race, a sort of Tour de Foothills in the Traveler's Rest area. The shopping district, for pedestrians only, will include specialty shops carrying such diverse wares as antiques, gifts, sporting goods, and ladies clothing. A wine and cheese shop and a bakery will add to the complement of restaurants and cafes.

As with any town, it takes time. At Crescent Mountain Vineyards, the vision is already in place, and soon, the reality will be as well.

Directions to Crescent Mountain Vineyards
From Greenville, South Carolina take U. S. Highway 25 north to State Road 11 (also called the Cherokee Foothills Scenic Highway). Stay on Highway 25, go under the overpass and take the first right at the sign that says Crescent Valley Farms. Go 1/2 mile and Crescent Mountain Vineyards is on your right.

From Asheville, North Carolina take Interstate 26 south to Exit 22. From there, take U. S. Highway 25 south into South Carolina. From the state line, go about 6 miles. Just before you reach the overpass of State Road 11, turn left at the sign that says Crescent Valley Farms. Crescent Mountain Vineyards is ½ mile on the right.

While You're Here

Located in the northwestern most part of the state, you can easily cross back and forth from South to North Carolina to find museums, attractions, shopping and outdoor activities. With lots of history, and lots of gorgeous scenery, this area is known South Carolina's Upcountry.

Greenville County, South Carolina
Greater Greenville Convention and Visitors Bureau
206 S. Main Street
Greenville, SC 29601
(800) 351-7180 (toll free), (864) 421-0000, Fax (864) 421-0005

Poinsett Bridge
From U. S. Highway 25 N, 2 miles NW of SC 11, turn onto Old U.S. 25 and go 3.2 miles. Turn right onto Callahan Mountain Road. The bridge is 2.2 miles on the left
This old road, built in 1820, was the early link between Greenville and Asheville. The stone-arch bridge is a graceful relic of a mason's art and the oldest bridge in the state.

Jones Gap and Mountain Bridge Recreation and Wilderness Area
Off U. S. Highway 276 and SC 11 on River Falls Road, northwest of Cleveland
Named for pioneer Solomon Jones whose early road to North Carolina traversed the Middle Saluda River Gorge. This is a river and wilderness centered park with the trail head for the Jones Gap Trail, a five mile hike to Caesar's Head. Picnicking, early fish hatchery, interpretive center, primitive camping.
(864) 836-3647

Paris Mountain State Park
Off U. S. Highway 25 on State Park Road north of Greenville
Paris Mountain has been a protected area since 1890 and offers both modern and primitive camping, lake swimming, fishing ponds, pedal boats, hiking trails and picnicking.
(864) 244-5565

Caesar's Head and Raven Cliff Falls
U. S. Highway 276 near the North Carolina state line
At 3,208 feet, this park, is one of the high spots in the state, literally. It

boasts rocky promontories, a visitors center and hiking trails. A two mile trail takes you to Raven Cliff Falls.
(864) 836-6115

Bed & Breakfast Inns in Greenville

Creekside Plantation
3118 South Hwy 14
Greenville, SC 29615
(864) 297-3293
Web site: www.bbonline.com/sc/creekside/

Pettigru Place Bed & Breakfast
302 Pettigru Street
Greenville, SC 29615
(864) 242-4529

Henderson County, North Carolina
Henderson County Travel & Tourism Department
201 S. Main Street/P. O. Box 721
Hendersonville, NC 28792/28793
(800) 828-4244 (toll free), (828) 693-9708, Fax (828) 697-4996

Hendersonville
Historic Hendersonville
Listed on the National Register of Historic Places. Lively restored downtown with shops, antique stores and restaurants.
(828) 697-2022

Western North Carolina Air Museum
1340 Gilbert Street/P. O. Box 2343
Hendersonville, NC 28792/28793
First air museum in the state features award winning restored, replica, antique and vintage airplanes. Regular flights from a grass field at the museum
(828) 698-2482

Wolfe's Angel
U. S. Highway 64 West at Oakdale Cemetery
Author Thomas Wolfe's first novel was "Look Homeward Angel" in which there are numerous references to an angel statue. This is the statue.
(828) 693-9708

Bed & Breakfast Inns in Hendersonville

Apple Inn
1005 White Pine Drive
Hendersonville, NC 28739
(800) 615-6611 (toll free), (828) 693-0107
Web site: www.appleinn.com

Mountain Home Bed & Breakfast
10 Courtland Blvd.
Hendersonville, NC 28758
(800) 397-0066 (toll free), (828) 697-9090, Fax (828) 698-2477
Web site: www.mountainhomeinn.com

Westhaven Bed & Breakfast
1235 5th Avenue, West
Hendersonville, NC 28739-4111
(828) 693-8791

Flat Rock
Connemara - Carl Sandburg Home National Historic Site
1928 Little River Road
Flat Rock, NC 28731
American poet, historian, author and lecturer Carl Sandburg spent the final 22 years of his life at this estate.
(828) 693-4178
Web site: www.nps.gov.carl/

Flat Rock Playhouse, The State Theatre of North Carolina
2661 Greenville Highway
Flat Rock, NC 28731
Considered one of the best summer stock theatres in the country, it has presented professional productions for more than 50 years.
(828) 693-0731, Fax (828) 693-6795

Flat Rock Historic District
Included on the National Register of Historic Places. Began in the mid 19th century as a summer retreat for affluent planters and businessmen from Charles, South Carolina and Europe

Bed & Breakfast Inns in Flat Rock

Flat Rock Inn Bed & Breakfast
2810 Greenville Highway
Flat Rock, NC 28731
(800) 266-3996 (toll free), (828) 696-3273
Web site: www.bbhost.com/flatrockinn

The Woodfield Inn
2905 Greenville Highway
Flat Rock, NC 28731
(800) 533-6016 (toll free), (828) 693-6016
Web site: www.woodfieldinn.com

From Crescent Mountain Vineyards, visitors can see the Blue Ridge Mountains.

Ideas For Touring

Here are some ideas for creating your own mini-tours of the Carolina wineries and their local attractions.

Western Carolinas Wine Tour

Silohouse in Waynesville, NC
Biltmore Estate Winery in Asheville, NC
Teensy Winery in Union Mills, NC
Crescent Mountain Vineyards in Travelers Rest, SC

Base yourself in Asheville for a week or more of fun. Visit the four Carolina mountain wineries, all with breathtaking scenery and all less than an hour's drive away. All of the wineries produce Vitis vinifera wines, from bold Cabernet Sauvingnons at Silohouse to crisp Chardonnays at Crescent Mountain Vineyards (look for the 1998 vintage to be released). Lots of history, beautiful scenery, shopping and outdoor activities will keep you busy. Allow a whole day or more for Biltmore Estate. See poet Carl Sandburg's home near East Flat Rock, NC. Chimney Rock is worth the climb, with lots of quaint mountain shops in the village below. Take the Blue Ridge Parkway to Mount Mitchell State Park, the highest elevation in the Eastern United States. Maggie Valley, Cherokee, the Pisgah National Forest and the Great Smokey Mountains National Park are all close by. Lots of photo opportunities. There's more to do here than you can possibly do, so choose the activities that suit you. Picnicking, hiking and dipping your feet in chilly mountain waterfalls make wonderful memories.

Piedmont Wine Tour

Waldensian Heritage Wines, Valdese, NC
North Carolina Waldensian Products, Hickory, NC
Westbend Vineyards, Lewisville, NC
Germanton Winery, Germanton, NC

Travel east to west or west to east, but don't miss any of this tour. Learn the difference between Waldensian Heritage wines and Waldensian Style wines. Sample a variety of wines from German style wines to Muscadine all in one locale. Some of North Carolina's lesser known history comes alive here in the settlements of the French speaking Italian Waldensians in

Valdese to the Moravians of German-ancestry in Olde Salem. Beautiful scenery, lots of shopping (furniture shopping from Hickory to High Point is the ultimate), fine art, state parks, Pisgah National Forest, Grandfather Mountain and the Blue Ridge Parkway are all within easy reach. Take a break from your wine tour and visit the Strohs Brewery in Winston-Salem. Lots to see and do here.

Carolinas Connection Wine Tour

Montmorenci Vineyards, Montmorenci, SC
Cruse Vineyards, Chester, SC
Dennis Vineyards, Albemarle, NC

Get a closer look at both Carolinas on this tour. From barrel fermented Chardonnays to rich Chambourcins to dry Muscadines, this tour offers vino variety. Start in Aiken, South Carolina for history, horses, hiking, Montmorenci and more. Sumpter National Forest is nearby as well as state parks, restaurants and shopping. Head north to Chester, South Carolina in the Olde English District for history, shopping, Cruse Vineyards and another section of the Sumpter National Forest. Stay on I-77 north to Charlotte then head east to Albemarle for Dennis Vineyards. Lots to do in the Charlotte area from Discovery Place hands-on science museum to the Charlotte Motor Speedway. The Uwharrie National Forest offers camping and outdoor activities. Buy your wine as you go. State laws prohibit the shipping of wine from state to state, but you can purchase wine at the wineries and take it with you.

Coastal Carolinas Wine Tour

Martin Vineyard, Knotts Island, NC
Bennett Vineyards, Edward NC
Duplin Wine Cellars, Rose Hill, NC
La Belle Amie, Little River, SC
Truluck Vineyards, Lake City, SC

This is a big bite for one tour, but if you have the time and like to drive, it's well worth it. Travel the beaches, ride the ferries and experience the Outer Banks. Martin Vineyards offers a vine-land variety from Chardonnay to fruit wines. Bennett Vineyards offers estate bottled Muscadine wines and u-pick grapes in season. Duplin Wine Cellars offers dinner shows and a large selection of Muscadine wines and gifts from their extensive wine shop. La Bell Amie and Truluck are expecting vinifera vintages in 1999, so call before going. This is where America and the American wine industry began. Long before anyone even knew there was a California, native grape vines grew wild. Look for huge old vines in every backyard in the coastal plain. Wild vines can be found in the Croatan National Forest and the Hoffman Forest in Onslow County. Beaches, beaches and more beaches await you, as well as history in Elizabeth City, Roanoke Island (the outdoor drama The Lost Colony has been running for more than 60 years during the summer months), Bath, New Bern and Wilmington, North Carolina. Lots and lots to do.

U-Pick Vineyards in North Carolina

Beaufort County
Bennett Vineyards
Buddy Harrell
6832 Bonnerton Road
Edward, North Carolina 27821
(252) 322-7154

Bladen County
Johnson Farm
Dean & Carl Johnson
Highway 210 - 18956 East
Ivanhoe, NC 28447
(910) 669-2712

Hardwick's Vineyard
Ray & Elma Lee Hardwick
610 Ham Road
Elizabethtown, NC 28337
(910) 862-3136

Alex Gooden Vineyard
Alex Gooden
P. O. Box 1242
Elizabethtown, NC 28337
(910) 862-4761

Ed Mote Vineyard
J. E. Mote
317 Mote Field Road
Harrells, NC 28444
(910) 588-4829

Carter Farms Vineyard
Ralph & Doris Carter
11671 Hwy. 701 North
Garland, NC 28441
(910) 588-4932

Brunswick County
Indigo Farms (Strawberries)
Bellamy Family
1542 Hickman Road, NW
Calabash, NC 28467
(910) 287-6794, (910) 287-6403

Cleveland County
Killdeer Farm
Ervin & Debbie Lineberger
300 Goforth Road
Kings Mountain, NC 28086
(704) 739-6602

Currituck County
Martin Vineyards
David & Jeannie Martin
P. O. Box 186
Knotts Island, NC 27950
(252) 429-3542

Durham County
Herndon Hills Farm
Nancy Herndon
7110 Massey Chapel Road
Durham, NC 27713
(919) 544-1235

Edgecomb County
Taylor farm
Jim & Peggy Taylor
Rte. 1, Box 650
Tarboro, NC 27886
(252) 641-9122

Franklin County
Windmill Vineyards
Don & Arlene DeJong
428 Husketh Road
(behind Hill Ridge Farm)
Youngsville, NC 27596
(919) 556-4078

Benton Grove Vineyards
Furnie & Shirley Cahoon, Mgrs.
1624 Sledge Road
Louisburg, NC 27549
(919) 497-0910

Greene County
Martha's Vineyard
Martha Bottoms
Rte. 2, Box 94
Stantonsburg, NC 27883
(252) 238-2279

Dixie Green Vineyard
Bert Dixon
P. O. Box 235, Hwy 903 E.
Maury, NC 28554
(252) 747-5555

Guilford County
Birch Creek Vineyards
Worth Jones
7845 Hwy 68 North
Stokesdale, NC 27357
(336) 288-6919

Carl Garrett's Vineyard
Carl & Connie Garrett
5409 Coble Church Road
Julian, NC 27283
(336) 697-8013

Harnett County
John Mason's Vineyard
John & Mildred Mason
1934 Old U. S. 421
Lillington, NC 27546
(910) 893-4771

Johnston County
Hinnant Farms Vineyard
Glenn P. Creech and
R. Willard Hinant
P. O. Box 189
Pine Level, NC 27568
(919) 965-3350

Lenoir County
Loftin's Berry Farm
W. Dennis Loftin, and
Don & Dan King
1331 Hwy. 58 South
Kinston, NC 28501
(252) 522-5086

Montgomery County
The Earl Orchard
Ed & Betty Lou Burton
P. O. Box 217, Hwy 211
Candor, NC 27229
(910) 673-2757

Nash County
Lotis Langley Vineyard
Lotis W. & Lorraine Langley
6330 Vaughan Chapel Road
Nashville, NC 27856
(252) 937-6350

Pender County
Bannerman Vineyard
Bannerman Family
2624 Stag Park Road
Burgaw, NC 28425
(910) 259-5474

Randolph County
Hill's Orchard
Hubert & Betty Hill
3452 Marvin Hill Place
Trinity, NC 27370
(336) 475-7042

Rockingham County
A. B. Gilliam, Jr. Farm
A. B. Gilliam
771 NC 150
Reidsville, NC 27320
(336) 349-3158

Sampson County
Sir Charles Vineyards
Charles & Louise Daughtry
3548 Wrye Branch Road
Newton Grove, NC 28366
(910) 567-6290

Wake County
Cook's Vineyard
Leslie G. Cook
Rte. 2, Box 202
Zebulon, NC 27597
(919) 496-5673

Greenleaf Farm and Nursery
John & Dianne Earp
6279 Applewhite Road
Wendell, NC 27591
(919) 365-6348

The Vineyard
David & Sheila Rohrbach
4300 Old Milburnie Road
Raleigh, NC 27604
(919) 266-4033

North Carolina Woman Makes Spirited Crafts With Wine Bottles

For Martha McDavid Wilson, a ghost of an idea is all it takes to get her creative juices flowing. In fact, she has a very spirited art hobby. She makes ghosts.

Using cheesecloth soaked in a fabric stiffening solution, Martha drapes dolls and artist's model forms, creating ethereal but solid representations of light and air beings. Nothing escapes her keen eye and sense of humor when it comes to details and ideas, even the Ghost of an Idea, a little ghost holding a light bulb.

Martha lives in Farmville, North Carolina with her mother, artist Alice Harper McDavid. In fact the whole McDavid clan are artists including her sisters "Poo", who makes bread dough baskets and Lis, who paints. The kitchen walls of the rambling brick ranch are adorned with still life paintings by Alice and her late husband Jack's grandmother.

"I started out majoring in Biology," explains Martha. "I loved Biology, especially genetics, but switched majors and ended up in Art School, but Daddy always said I should have been a writer." Martha has a Bachelor of Fine Arts degree in Interior Design with a Minor in Crafts from East Carolina University.

After moving around a lot, 13 jobs and two children later, Martha found herself working as the commercial artist in a toy factory. She enjoyed the job which gave her a chance to write more than she had before. Then the first of two heart attacks and a ruptured disc at the back of her neck put her on the disabled list.

"I've never not worked and it about drove me crazy." says Martha. "I started thinking what could I do? Whatever it was it had to be something that I could do in brief spans of time. The ruptured disc causes my arms to go to sleep if I work at something too long."

She had always done crafts or artwork of some kind and had made a few of the little ghosts. She liked working on them so she started producing more of them, gathering ideas from various sources. Cliches were the obvious first ideas. There's the Ghost of an Idea, and School Spirit rendered two ghosts, one with a football and pompom and one wearing a mortar board and brandishing a diploma. The Ghost of Christmas Present carries presents to all good little ghosts, and the Guardian Angel is a Heavenly Spirit.

Martha's newest collection is called Wine Spirits which she makes using the same technique and attaching the ghosts to wine bottles. One ghost lounges on a horizontal bottle, one hugs the bottle neck, and one leans against the bottle carrying a sign that says "Let's Party". Other ideas include a pirate with a eye patch sitting on a bottle. Each one is different, and like all her ghosts, no two are alike, even the bottles.

"I don't drink wine so I have to get my bottles from friends, but my biggest problem is finding the cheesecloth. I need to buy it by the yard, and places where I used to get it don't carry it anymore."

Other supplies and materials that are more easily attained run the gamut from tiny sea shells for the Grey Man of Hatteras to a slender length of chain for a traditional chain rattling graveyard ghost. Martha haunts craft stores, yard sales and discount stores for ghostly accessories.

Inspiration comes from many sources as well. "Sometimes I just sit around and think and I start going 'a ghost of this and a spirit of that'. Sometimes the materials give me an idea and sometimes it's a matter of the little model talking to me and saying 'Hey, I want to be so-and-so'. Mama says I'm obsessed."

That may be true. Martha says everywhere she goes she buys ghost story books in search of new ghosts to make. Her collection of colored ghosts come from all over the world, each with it's own tale. The Pink Lady, the Gray Lady, the Green Lady of Ireland and the Laughing Black Ghost are just a few. She also gets inspiration in cemeteries.

"Graveyard stomping can be extremely interesting. The things that are written on tombstones will slay you. It can be a lot of fun if you're interested in that sort of thing. I was always told I had a morbid sense of humor, but I never knew it would lead me to graveyards in my 'old age'."

Martha says she gets ideas from the stories of people who are buried there as well as just picking up stories in her travels. One such tale is of a ghost in New Bern, North Carolina who leaves pennies on a hearth.

Martha is writing a book on how to make the little ghosts. They are copyrighted as Fabric Sculptures. She says they're easy to make and take about 45 minutes. Drying time for the material is up to 24 hours. Glitter and food coloring can be added to the solution to create different effects. For ideas, Martha says focus on your hobbies and interests, or for gifts, on the hobbies and interests of others. You could do the Spirit of Music, for instance. The most important thing in the creative process, says Martha is to be open to materials and accessories that work for you.

Martha's first showing of the little ghosts was sponsored by the Farmville Arts Council. The Martha McDavid Wilson Spirited Art Show was held during the month of October, a most appropriate time for ghostly encounters.

"The other night I was up late typing something and I heard the house creaking and thought 'Mama's asleep, there's nobody else here. The ghosts have come alive and they're moving around the house'."

As if there's a ghost of a chance of that happening!

School Spirits are another line of ghostly creatures created by Martha Wilson.

Wild, Wonderful Wine Recipes

Wine is a wonderful, versatile cooking ingredient that no kitchen should be without. Use your imagination. Try different wines to create different flavors in the same recipes.

1. Use wine in place of part of the liquid in preparing:
    dry sauce and gravy mixes
    cake batters, cookie doughs, puddings or pie fillings
    homemade and condensed soups
    stews and smothered steak
    gelatin desserts or salads
2. After sautéing meat, pour a few tablespoons of wine into the same pan and combine it with any browned particles left from the cooking. Pour over meat and serve.
3. Add wine when reheating leftover meat, fish or poultry dishes.
4. Choose complementary wines to pour over fresh, frozen or canned fruits.
5. For low fat cooking, sauté or stir fry vegetables in red or white wine instead of oil or butter.
6. Use dry white wine in place of water when microwaving frozen vegetables.

Quick Low Fat Veggie-Pasta Entree
1/2 cup yellow squash
1/2 cup zucchini
1/2 cup onion
1/2 cup red bell pepper
1/2 cup mushrooms
2 to 3 tablespoons red or white wine
2 cups cooked noodles or angel hair pasta
Fat free grated Parmesan cheese

Cut vegetables into one inch pieces. Sauté in wine until vegetables are tender and wine is absorbed. Spoon vegetables over cooked pasta and sprinkle with Parmesan cheese. Makes two servings.

Marinated Green Beans

1/4 cup dry red wine
1/3 cup lemon juice
3 tablespoons extra virgin olive oil
1/2 teaspoon celery salt
3/4 teaspoon dried dill weed
3 tablespoons finely minced onion
1/8 cup slivered almonds
1 1/2 pounds fresh or frozen green beans, cooked to taste and drained

Heat wine and lemon juice. Add oil and seasonings; pour over cooked green beans. Cover and chill thoroughly, turning occasionally to mix marinade with the beans. Serve chilled. Makes 5 to 6 servings.

(Variation: Add dark and light red kidney beans and wax beans for a bean salad. Increase the marinade ingredients depending on how many more beans you add.)

Fried Cabbage

(courtesy Mrs. Patty Stewart)
4 strips of bacon, diced
2 cloves crushed garlic
1 large onion, sliced
2 pounds sliced cabbage
1/2 cup chicken broth
1/2 cup dry white wine

In a large skillet or Dutch oven, sauté bacon until cooked, not crisp. Add garlic and onion. Sauté until onion is clear. Add cabbage, chicken broth and wine. Cook covered until cabbage collapses, about 5 minutes. Remove lid and cook until liquid is reduced and cabbage is tender. Do not over cook cabbage.

Baked Apples

(courtesy Ann Ashley, Guest Services Manager, Biltmore Estate Winery)
Quarter Granny Smith apples into a baking dish
Sprinkle with brown sugar and cinnamon and dot with butter
Add 2 cups of Biltmore Estate Johannisberg Riesling
Cover and bake at 350 degrees until apples are soft
(The alcohol bakes off leaving only the wine flavor.)

Grape Juice Sherbet Float

1 quart pineapple or lime sherbet
1 1/3 cups fresh strawberries, blueberries, peaches or other seasonal fruit
fresh or sparkling Scuppernong grape juice

Spoon sherbet equally into 4 stemmed glasses. Top each with 1/3 cup sliced fruit. Just before serving, pour 1 to 2 tablespoons grape juice over the top. Makes 4 servings.

Scuppernong Grape Ice

2/3 cup sugar
1 1/2 cups water
1 cup lemon juice
1/4 cup orange juice
1 cup fresh Scuppernong grape juice or sparkling Scuppernong grape juice

Combine sugar and water in a heavy saucepan. Bring to a boil, stirring frequently. Boil 5 minutes. Remove from heat and add remaining ingredients, stirring well. Cool. Pour mixture into a flat tray or pan. Freeze until mixture reaches consistency of a sherbet, stirring occasionally during freezing. Scoop into sherbet dishes and serve. Makes about 1 quart.

Wine Sauce

(courtesy Mrs. Patty Stewart)
1 cup sugar
1/2 cup butter
1/2 cup red wine
In a large, heat resistant mixing bowl, beat butter and sugar until light. Heat wine in saucepan until just hot. <u>Do Not Boil</u>. Add to butter and sugar mixture. Place mixing bowl in a larger bowl or pan of hot water and stir for two minutes. Serve over plum pudding or fruit cake.

Red Delicious Punch

(courtesy North Carolina Waldensian Products)

Pour 2 bottles of Sparkling Apple Cider into a punch bowl, Mix in one quart of cranberry juice. Float a frozen ice ring and garnish with sprigs of mint.

Blushed Pineapples

(courtesy North Carolina Waldensian Products)

Mix 2 parts Sparkling Scuppernong Blush Cider with one part pineapple juice. Serve cold.

Magnolia Wine Spritzer

(courtesy Duplin Wine Cellars)

Mix equal parts of Duplin Wine Cellars Magnolia wine, lemonade, and 7-Up. Add ice and top with fruit (grapes, cherries, lemon slices, blue berries, use your imagination).

Florida Sangria

1 bottle (750 ml) of dry red wine
1 Florida orange, thinly sliced
1 lemon thinly sliced
1/2 cup sugar (optional)
1 (28 ounce) bottle Club Soda or 7-Up

Combine the wine, fruit and sugar in a large glass pitcher and let set one hour at room temperature. Just before serving, add the Club Soda or 7-Up and serve over ice. Makes 6 (8 ounce) servings.

Wine Jelly

3 cups sugar
2 cups dry red wine
1 (3 ounce) package liquid pectin

Combine sugar and wine in a large saucepan or Dutch oven. Cook over medium heat; stir until sugar dissolves (do not boil). Remove from heat, stir in pectin. Skim off foam with metal spoon. Quickly pour hot jelly into sterilized jars. Cover and process in boiling water bath for 5 minutes. Makes 4 half pints

Stir Fry Sauce
(courtesy Mrs. Patty Stewart)
one 15 ounce bottle of soy sauce
1 1/2 cups dry white wine
1/2 cup dry sherry
1/3 cup packed brown sugar
2 cloves garlic, cut in half
2 tablespoons chicken flavored granules
2 tablespoons grated fresh ginger root
2 teaspoons black peppercorns
1 1/2 teaspoons sesame oil

Combine all ingredients, cover and refrigerate for 8 hours. Pour through a large mesh strainer, discarding solids. Pour into bottles or jars and store in refrigerator up to 3 months. Dress up the bottles or jars for gift giving. Great for marinating chicken or pork, grilling or wok cooking. Yield 4 1/2 cups.

Appendix A - Numbers You Need

North Carolina Division of Tourism, Film and Sports Development
(For the state Official Travel Guide and other information)
301 North Wilmington Street
Raleigh, North Carolina 27601-2825
(800) VISIT NC (toll free), (919) 733-8372, Fax (919) 733-8582
Web site: www.visitnc.com

North Carolina Division of Archives and History
Historical Publications Section
(For a catalog of publications available and other information)
109 East Jones Street
Raleigh, North Carolina, 27601-2807
(919) 733-7442, Fax (919) 733-1439
Web site: www.ah.dcr.state.nc.us/sections/hp/default.htm

South Carolina Department of Parks, Recreation and Tourism
(For the South Carolina Travel Guide and other information)
P. O. Box 71
Columbia, South Carolina 29202
(803) 734-1700, Fax (803) 734-0138
Web site: www.travelsc.com

South Carolina Video Adventures
(For a free catalog of South Carolina historical, cultural and environmental
VHS tapes)
(800) 553-7752 (toll free)
Web site: www.scetv.org/scetv/mkthome.html

South Carolina State Parks
(For general information and for their brochure Cabins/Camping & Other
Facilities)
1205 Pendleton Street
Columbia, South Carolina 29201
(888) 88-PARKS (toll free), (803) 734-0156, Fax (803) 734-1017
Web site: www.southcarolinaparks.com

Appendix B - Wine on the Web

Woodhaven Publishing   **www.NCBooks.com**
Home of <u>Carolina Wine Country</u> *The Complete Guide*. Order books and check out the links. Under construction at the time of printing this book.

NC Grapes & Wine (North Carolina Grape Council)
www.agr.state.nc.us/markets/commodit/horticul/grape
Provides links to NC Wine Page, Winery Map, Grape & Wine History, Grape Growing and Events. A grape place to start surfing for Carolina wine.

NC Wines
www.agr.state.nc.us/markets/commodit/horticul/grape/winepg.htm
NC Winery Map, Types of Wines, Home Wine Making and Juicy Links

Biltmore Estate Winery   **www.biltmore.com/Dmain.html**
Tells all about the winery with links to the main Biltmore Estate home page. You can check out wine production and the wine Tasting Room, browse the Biltmore wine list, and view upcoming events.

Crescent Mountain Vineyards   **www.cmvineyard.com**
Photographs of the French village in the South Carolina Upcountry, what's to come, updates and more. A new site that is constantly changing.

Germanton Gallery and Winery   **www.germantongallery.com**
Winner of the Surfer's Choice Blue Diamond Award, this is a graphically heavy site, but it loads pretty quickly. Walk through the art gallery and the sculpture gallery and view the latest art offerings. Peruse the wine cellar for current vintages. Order on-line. More rooms are being added all the time. A well maintained site.

North Carolina Waldensian Products   **www.waldensian.com**
Prepare for a delightful surprise as you open this site (be sure your sound is on). Tells all about the Waldensian Winery and wines, with links to Wine & Health

Westbend Vineyards
www.agr.state.nc.us/markets/commodit/horticul/grape/westbend.htm
Tells all about Westbend, pictures and ordering information.

Ford's Fancy Fruits & Gourmet Foods
www.TheNCStore.com
Known as the North Carolina Store. Retailer of North Carolina products, including North Carolina wines and jams made from Scuppernong grapes. Online ordering.

Juicy Links
www.agr.state.nc.us/markets/commodit/horticul/grape/winelink.htm
Information packed site about North Carolina wines and wines in general. Covers Wine shops, US Wine Regions, Agricultural Links, Noteworthy North Carolina Travel Links, Food Links, Wine and Health Links, Wine Making Links, and North Carolina Winery Links. Also has a chat room and more wine info.

North Carolina Grape Council Wine and Health Page
www.agr.state.nc.us/markets/commodit/horticul/grape/wineheal.htm
Lots of links to articles about wine and health.

Smartwine Wine and Health Page
http://smartwine.com/fp/fphome.htm
Articles on the health benefits of wine, including the 60 Minutes French Paradox revisited text.

Bibliography

Brenner, Leslie & Teague, Lettie. <u>Fear of Wine: An Introductory Guide to the Grape</u>. New York, NY: Bantam Books, 1995

Dufur, Brett. <u>Exploring Missouri Wine Country</u>. Rocheport, MO: Pebble Publishing, 1997 (800) 576-7322

Jones, Frank. <u>The Save Your Heart Wine Guide</u>. New York, NY: St. Martin's Press, 1996

Perdue, Lewis. <u>The French Paradox and Beyond: Living Longer With Wine and the Mediterranean Lifestyle</u> .

Rainbird, George. <u>An Illustrated Guide to Wine</u>. London, England; Octopus Books Limited, 1987

Wager, Phillip. <u>Grapes Into Wine: a guide to Wine Making in America</u>. New York, NY: Knopf: distributed by Random House, 1976

Wine Glossary

Acid, Acidity: sharp, tart effect of fruit on both the nose and tongue. Healthy grapes contain natural acidity which gives the wine its crisp, refreshing quality.

American hybrids: native grapes developed from American root stock

Aroma: perfume of fresh fruit; diminishes with fermentation and disappears with age to be replaced by the bouquet.

Balanced: having all natural elements in harmony.

Big: full of body and flavor; high degree of color, alcohol, and acidity

Blanc du Boise: a French-American hybrid grape developed in Florida

Body: weight and substance of wine in the mouth; actually a degree of viscosity dependent on percentage of alcoholic and sugar content. Wines are referred to as light-bodied or full-bodied, etc.

Bouquet: fragrance that a mature wine gives off when opened; it develops further in the glass.

Brix (bricks): a scale that measures the sugar content in the juice of the grape before fermentation.

Cabernet Sauvignon: a red vinifera grape associated with the Bordeaux region in France. Often tannic when young requiring both barrel and bottle aging to soften it. Wines are complex and age well.

Cabernet Franc: similar to, and often blended with, Cabernet Sauvignon. Usually lighter in body, Cabernet Franc has a deep purple color when young and a perfumey aroma.

Carlos: a white Muscadine grape commonly called a Scuppernong.

Catawba: a white labrusca-type grape that produces sweet white wines with a distinct foxy character. In recent years it is also made into dry and sparkling wines.

Cayuga (ki-u-ga): A white American hybrid varietal developed in New York state that produces a light-bodied, fruity, semi-dry wine. Also called Savannah White.

Chambourcin (sham-bor-sin): a red French-American varietal that produces a soft, fruity, light-bodied, dry wine. A relative new-comer, Chambourcin has only been available commercially since 1963.

Chardonnay: a white vinifera grape that produces a dry white wine with a fruity character. It is often barrel fermented with noticeable oak flavors and aromas.

Clarity: wine should have a clear color; it should not have cloudiness or visible particles.

Clean: a well-constituted wine with no offensive smell or taste.

Concord: a red labrusca-type grape that produces a dry to semi-dry wine.

Dry: completely lacking sugar or sweetness; not to be confused with bitterness or sourness.

Estate: 100% grapes from a winery-owned vineyard.

Fat: full-bodied but flabby. In white wines it is often due to too much residual sugar. In red wines, it means softness and maturity.

Fermentation: the process by which yeast, combined with sugar and must, produces alcohol.

Finish: taste that wines leave in the mouth, whether pleasant or unpleasant.

Flat: dull, unattractive, low in acidity. The next stage after flabby. In sparkling wines, wine that has lost its sparkle.

Fortified wine: a wine that has had brandy or spirits added, such as Port, Sherry or Madeira.

Foxy: pronounced flavor in wines made from native American grapes usually found in young wines.

French-American hybrids: grapes that are crosses between Vitis Vinifera and native American species. First developed in France in the 1800's, these grapes combine the disease resistance and winter hardiness of American species with the classic flavors of the European species.

Fruity: aroma and flavor from fresh grapes found usually in young wines.

Full bodied: a big wine with high alcoholic content and extract such as a mouth filling table wine.

Heavy: over endowed with alcohol, more than full bodied; lacking finesse.

Legs: the droplets that form and ease down the sides of the glass when the wine is swirled.

Light: referring to body; low alcohol content, usually young and fruity.

Magnolia: a white Muscadine grape

Medium dry: some residual sugar left. Not completely dry

Melody: a white American hybrid grape developed at Cornell University.

Merlot: a red Bordeaux-type vinifera grape that produces wines similar to Cabernet Sauvignon, with which it is often blended. These wines mature earlier than Cabernet Sauvignon and may be enjoyed as younger wines.

Muscadine: native grape found growing wild in North Carolina. White varieties are called locally by the term Scuppernong. Purple or black varieties are commonly called Muscadines.

Must: grape juice in the vat before it is converted into wine.

Niagara: a large greenish-white American hybrid with a tough skin and sweet flavor.

Nesbitt: a red Muscadine grape

Noble: a red Muscadine grape

North Carolina Wine: wine that has 85% North Carolina grown grapes

Nose: the overall smell of wine

Oak, Oaky: a smell and taste derived from fermentation in small oak casks.

Oenology: the study of wine and wine making

Phylloxera (fill-locs-era): a aphid, or louse, that destroys vineyards by eating vine roots.

Ripe: can refer to grapes, smell and taste

Sauvignon Blanc: a white vinifera grape associated with the Bordeaux region of France. When grown in warmer climates, the flavors and aromas lean more toward spice, pear and citrus.

Scuppernong: the name given to the original variety of bronze colored Muscadine grapes

Seyval Blanc (say-val blonk): a white French-American varietal. Makes a dry to semi-dry, crisp, light-bodied, fruity wine. Dry versions are sometimes described as being like a French Chablis.

Soft: a mellow wine usually low in acid and tannin.

Spice: definite aroma and flavor of spice from certain grape varieties.

Suwanee: a white American hybrid grape

Sweet: having high residual sugar content, either from the grapes themselves or from added sugar or from the stopping of fermentation.

Tannin: an essential preservative extracted from the skins of red grapes during fermentation. It dries the mouth.

Unfortified: naturally fermented. Sugars can be added, but the alcohol content cannot exceed 17%.

Varietal: distinctive aroma and taste derived from a specific grape variety.

Vintage: 95% grapes from the particular year the wine was made.

Vintner: wine maker; one who deals in wines

Viticulture: the art and science of growing grapes

Vitis labrusca: considered the American "bunch" grapes, or the American version of vinifera. Wines made from these grapes offer intense, fruity flavors.

Vitis rotundifolia: large round grapes that are native to the Carolina coast are Muscadines, known locally as Scuppernongs. They are commonly eaten fresh or made into wines and jellies. Wines of this grape are rich, full-flavored, and very fruity.

Vitis vinifera: traditional European species of grapes that produce European or California-style wines.

Index

Need more copies for family, friends or yourself.

Carolina Wine Country
The Complete Guide
By Pamela Watson

is available in bookstores, specialty shops and vineyards and wineries throughout the Carolinas. It may also be ordered directly from the publisher. Please call toll free and order with your credit card, or send this order form with full payment to:

104 Woodhaven Court
Greenville, North Carolina 27834

phone & fax   (252) 353-2800
toll free   (877) 353-2800

Carolina Wine Country
The Complete Guide
By Pamela Watson

Please send me _____ copies at $14.95 each = _____
    NC residents add 89¢ per book sales tax = _____
    Shipping ($2 first book, $1 each additional book) = _____

(Please Print Clearly)   **Total Order** =_____

Name _____
Address _____
City, State, Zip _____
Phone: (_____) _____
e-mail address _____

Check enclosed _____
Charge my credit card: _____ VISA _____ MasterCard
credit card # _____
expiration date _____/_____
Signature _____

(Please make checks payable to Woodhaven Publishing)

Carolina Wineries

Bennett Vineyards (Beaufort County, NC) (252) 322-7154

Biltmore Estate Winery (Buncombe County, NC) (800) 543-2961

Crescent Mountain Vineyards (Greenville County, SC)
(864) 836-VINE

Cruse Vineyards (Chester County, SC) (803) 377-3944

Dennis Vineyards (Stanly County, NC) (704) 982-6090

Duplin Wine Cellars (Duplin County, NC) (910) 289-3888

Germanton Vineyard & Winery (Stokes County, NC)
(336) 969-2075

La Belle Amie Vineyard (Horry County, SC) (843) 399-WINE

Martin Vineyards (Currituck County, NC) (252) 429-3542

Montmorenci Vineyards (Aiken County, SC) (803) 649-4870

North Carolina Waldensian Products (Catawba County, NC)
(828) 327-3867

Silohouse Vineyards (Haywood County, NC) (828) 452-9666

Teensy Winery (Rutherford County, NC) (828) 287-7763

Truluck Vineyards (Florence County, SC) (843) 389-0100

Waldensian Heritage Wines (Burke County, NC) (828) 879-3202

Westbend Vineyards (Forsyth County, NC) (336) 945-5032

While waiting for the wine to chill...

In computing wine production, some wine makers think in gallons and some think in cases. There are 2.38 gallons of wine in one case. Convert cases to gallons by multiplying by 2.38. Convert gallons to cases by dividing by 2.38.